The Secret Letters
of The Monk
Who Sold His
Ferrari

ALSO BY ROBIN SHARMA

*The Monk Who Sold His Ferrari*
*Leadership Wisdom from The Monk Who Sold His Ferrari*
*Discover Your Destiny with The Monk Who Sold His Ferrari*
*The Greatness Guide*
*Be Extraordinary: The Greatness Guide 2*

# The Secret Letters of The Monk Who Sold His Ferrari

ROBIN SHARMA

HarperElement
An Imprint of HarperCollins*Publishers*
77–85 Fulham Palace Road,
Hammersmith, London W6 8JB

www.harpercollins.co.uk

element and HarperElement are trademarks
of HarperCollins*Publishers* Ltd

First published in Canada by HarperCollins*Publishers* 2011
This edition 2011

1 3 5 7 9 10 8 6 4 2

Robin Sharma asserts the moral right to be identified
as the author of this work

A catalogue record of this book is available from the British Library

ISBN 978-0-00-732111-7

Printed and bound by Griffin Press, Australia

*Go as far as you can see. When you get there,*
*you'll be able to see farther.*
—Thomas Carlyle

# PROLOGUE

My wordless guide was moving quickly ahead of me, as if he too disliked being down here. The tunnel was damp, and dimly lit. The bones of six million Parisians were entombed in this place...

Suddenly the young man stopped at the entranceway of a new tunnel. It was separated from the one we had followed by a piece of rusted iron fencing. The tunnel was dark. My guide moved the fence to one side and turned into the blackness. He paused and looked behind at me, making sure I was following. I moved uncertainly out of the anemic light as his back disappeared in front of me. I took a few more steps. Then my foot knocked against something. A wooden rattle filled the air, and I froze. As I did, light flared around me. My guide had snapped on his flashlight.

*Suddenly I wished he hadn't. The gruesome orderliness was gone. Bones were everywhere—scattered across the floor around our feet, cascading from loose stacks against the walls. The glare from the flashlight caught on waves of dust and tendrils of cobwebs that hung from the ceiling.*

"Ça c'est pour vous," *said my guide. He thrust the flashlight at me. As I took it, he brushed past me.*

"What—" *I began to call out.*

*Before I could finish my question, the man snapped,* "Il vous rencontrera ici." *And then he was gone, leaving me alone, fifty feet underground, a solitary human being standing in a sea of the dead.*

# CHAPTER ONE

IT WAS ONE OF THOSE DAYS you find yourself wishing was over before you've got even ten minutes into it. It started when my eyes opened and I noticed an alarming amount of sunlight seeping in under the bedroom blinds. You know, an eight-a.m. amount of light—not a seven-a.m. amount of light. My alarm had not gone off. *That* realization was followed by twenty minutes of panicked cursing and shouting and crying (my six-year-old son did the crying) as I careened around the house, from bathroom to kitchen to front door, trying to gather all the ridiculous bits of stuff Adam and I needed for the rest of our day. As I pulled up in front of his school forty-five minutes later, Adam shot me a reproachful look.

"Mom says if you keep dropping me off late at school on Mondays, I won't be able to stay over Sunday nights anymore."

Oh, boy.

"Last time," I said. "Last time, I promise."

Adam was sliding out of the car now, a doubtful expression on his face.

"Here," I said, holding up a bulging plastic bag. "Don't forget your lunch."

"Keep it," Adam said, not looking at me. "I'm not allowed to bring peanut butter to school."

And then he turned on his heel and raced through the deserted school playground. *Poor kid,* I thought as I watched his little legs pumping toward the front door. Nothing worse than heading into school late, everyone already in class, the national anthem blaring through the hallways. *That* and no lunch to boot.

I threw the plastic bag onto the passenger seat and sighed. Another "custodial" weekend had come to an inglorious end. I had, apparently, failed spectacularly as a husband. Now it appeared that I would fail with equal flamboyance as a separated dad. From the moment I picked Adam up, I seemed to provide an unending series of disappointments. Despite the fact that all week I felt Adam's absence like a missing limb, I invariably arrived late on Fridays. The promised treat of pizza and a movie was dampened by the tuna sandwich that Annisha made Adam eat as his dinner hour came and went. And then there was my phone, which chirped incessantly, like it had a bad case of hiccups. It beeped during the movie, and when I was tucking Adam into bed. It beeped during our breakfast of slightly burned pancakes, and while we walked to the park. It beeped as we picked up takeout burgers, and all through story time. Of course the beeping wasn't the real problem. The real problem was that I kept picking the thing up. I checked my messages; I sent responses; I talked on the phone. And with each interruption, Adam became a little quieter, a little more distant. It broke my heart, yet the thought of ignoring the thing, or turning it off, made my palms sweat.

As I raced to work, I brooded about the botched weekend. When Annisha had announced that she wanted a trial separation, it felt like someone had backed over me with a truck. She had been complaining for years that I never spent time with her or Adam; that I was too caught up with work, too busy with my own life to be part of theirs.

"But how," I argued, "does leaving me fix any of that? If you want to see more of me, why are you making sure that you see *less?*"

She had, after all, said she still loved me. Said she wanted me to have a good relationship with my son.

But by the time I had moved into my own apartment, I was bruised and bitter. I had promised to try to spend more time at home. I had even begged off a company golf tournament and a client dinner. But Annisha said that I was only tinkering—I wasn't committed to fixing what was wrong. Every time I thought of those words, I clenched my teeth. Couldn't Annisha see how demanding my work was? Couldn't she see how important it was for me to keep moving ahead? If I hadn't been putting in the kind of hours I was, we wouldn't have our great house, or the cars, or the awesome big-screen TVs. Well, okay, I admit it—Annisha didn't give a damn about the TVs. But, still.

I made a promise to myself then—*I will be a great "separated dad."* I'll lavish attention on Adam; I'll go to all the school events; I'll be available to drive him to swimming or karate; I'll read him books. When he phones at night, I'll have all the time in the world to talk with him. I'll listen to his problems, give advice and share jokes. I'll help him with homework, and I'll even learn to play those annoying video games he likes. I'll have a wonderful relationship with my son, even if I can't have one with my wife. And I'll show Annisha that I'm not just "tinkering."

The first few weeks apart, I think I did pretty well. In some ways, it wasn't so hard. But I was shocked by how much I missed both of them. I would wake up in my apartment and listen for the tiny voice I knew wasn't there. I would pace around at night thinking, *This is the time when I might be reading a bedtime story. This is when I might give Adam his good-night hug.* And *This is the moment I would be crawling into bed with Annisha, the moment I would be holding her in my arms.* The weekends couldn't come soon enough for me.

But as the months ticked on, those thoughts began to fade. Or, more truly, they were crowded out by everything else. I would bring work home each evening or stay at work late. When Adam called, I'd be tapping away on my computer and hearing only every other sentence. Whole weeks would go by without me thinking once about what he might be doing during the days. When the school break came, I realized that I hadn't booked any time off to spend with him. Then I scheduled a client dinner on the night of Adam's spring school concert. I also forgot to take him for his six-month dental cleaning, even though Annisha had reminded me just the week before.

And I started to show up late on Fridays. This weekend was just another installment of "quality" time that was anything but.

I gave Danny, the security guard, a little wave as I pulled into the office parking lot. After my crazy rush to be here, I suddenly wished I wasn't. I pulled into my space, but I didn't turn off the engine right away.

In my defense, my obsession with work was completely natural. It was a highly stressful time at the company. Rumors had been flying for months that we were about to be sold. I had spent the last twelve weeks doing nothing but churning out reports: sales reports, inventory reports, staffing reports, profit-and-loss statements. When I closed my eyes at night, all I could see were the crowded grid lines of a spreadsheet. That was what awaited me inside the building, but I couldn't put it off any longer. I turned the engine off, grabbed my laptop case and headed in.

I said hello to Devin, our receptionist. His head was bent studiously over his computer screen, but I knew he was playing solitaire. As I veered right, I could see Devin smirking, but maybe I was just imagining that. The shortest route to my office is to the left, but I no longer went that way. Devin obviously thought that was because Tessa's desk was to the right. But that was only an added bonus. If I went to the right, I didn't have to go past Juan's office. *Juan.* Damn. I don't know why I should be bothered so much after all this time. It was only an unused office now. The blinds were up, the desk was clear, the chair was vacant. There were no pictures of Juan's wife and children on the filing cabinet, no coffee mugs on the credenza, no plaques on the wall. But it was as if the shadow of all those things hovered over the empty spaces.

I slowed my pace as I approached Tessa's cubicle. Tessa and I had worked together for years. We had always got along well—we shared the same sense of humor. I wasn't sure what was going to happen with Annisha, but I had to admit that I'd found myself thinking a lot about Tessa since the split.

I caught a glimpse of her dark hair, but she was on the phone. So I kept going.

Almost as soon as I was through my office door, I found myself turning around. I wondered if I should check out the new prototype before I started on more pressing work. I knew the design team would let me know about any developments, but the thought of distracting myself with a few minutes in the lab was tempting.

The design lab was where I'd started out. One of my first jobs was in the development sector of this place—an auto parts manufacturer. It was my dream job. Juan, the technical director, took me under his wing. Juan was my mentor.

But the thing is, even if you love your job, you can't stay put. That's a career killer. But no one had to *tell* me that. I was like a dog wagging my tail so hard that I'd put my back out. The people above noticed. When the next rung of the corporate ladder was offered to me, Juan took me into his office.

"You know," he said, "if you take this position, you'll be out of research and design for good. You'll be selling and managing. Is that what you want?"

"I want to move ahead, Juan," I said, laughing. "And I'm sure not going to wait for you to retire to do that!"

Juan gave me only a weak smile, but he didn't say anything else.

After that first step, I moved up through the ranks pretty

quickly. Now I was overseeing all our projects and product production for our biggest client.

I picked up my coffee mug, about to head down the hall to
the lab. But then I stopped. There was no need for me to be
there. I put my coffee cup down and dropped into my chair. I
snapped on my computer, opened a file and turned my eyes to
the maze of numbers that filled my screen.

A few hours later, I had just finished yet another profit-and-
loss statement and was about to return to my overflowing inbox,
when the phone rang. It took me a few seconds to recognize my
mother's voice. She sounded upset. *Good lord,* I thought. *Now
what?* My mother had been inordinately interested in my life in
recent months. It was beginning to annoy me.

"Sorry to have bothered you at work, Jonathan, but this is
important," she said. "I've just been talking with Cousin Julian,
and he needs to see you right away. It's urgent."

*Me?* I thought. *Why on earth would Cousin Julian need to see
me?*

To be frank, I didn't really know Cousin Julian. He wasn't my
cousin, but my mother's. She had been close with Julian and his
sister Catherine when they were all small, but I grew up on the
other side of the country. Far-flung relatives were as interesting
to me as last week's newspaper.

The only time I ever met Julian, I was about ten. We were
visiting Cousin Catherine, and she arranged a dinner at her
house. I don't recall whether Julian's wife was with him, or
whether he was already divorced. To tell you the truth, I don't
remember anything at all about the visit, except for one thing:
Julian's bright red Ferrari. I had heard Catherine mention it, so
I was waiting on the front steps when he peeled up the driveway.

The car was even more fabulous than I had pictured. Julian saw my face (my chin must have been scraping the top of my shoes), and he invited me for a ride. I had never been in a car that moved so fast. It felt as if, at any moment, the wheels might leave the pavement, and we would be airborne. I don't think I said a word the whole ride. When we arrived back at the house, Julian got out of the car, but I didn't move.

"You want to hang around in the car for a while?" he asked.

I nodded. He turned to leave but before he could go, I stopped him.

"Cousin Julian?"

"Yes," he said.

"How did you get this car?" I asked. "I mean . . . does it cost a lot of money?"

"It sure does," he said. "So if you want one of these yourself, Jonathan, you're going to have to work really, really hard when you grow up."

I never forgot that.

As I remember, Julian didn't stick around long after dinner—Mom and Cousin Catherine seemed disappointed, maybe a little annoyed. Although I was only ten, I could imagine that Julian had much more exciting places to be. He was clearly living the kind of life that I wanted when I got older. I watched with envy as Julian's fabulous sports car tore down the street.

After years of saying nothing about the man, Mom had begun to invoke Julian's name every time we got together. She had recently told me the Ferrari was long gone. Cousin Julian had, apparently, gone through some sort of life-changing experience. He'd quit his extremely lucrative job as a high-powered litigator, sold the Ferrari and embraced a "simple" existence. Mom said he had studied with a little-known group of monks who lived deep in the Himalayas and that he now often went around in a crimson robe. She said he was an utterly different man. I wasn't sure why she seemed to think this was such a good thing.

And she had been trying to get the two of us together. She had suggested that I make time to visit with him when I was in his city on business. But frankly, if I didn't have enough time for Annisha or Adam, why would I take a day off to spend with a man I hardly knew? Besides, if he'd still been a phenomenally successful lawyer with a glamorous lifestyle and a flashy sports car, I might have seen the point. But why did I need to spend time with an unemployed old man with no Ferrari? There were plenty of guys like him hanging around in my local bar.

"Mom," I said, "what are you talking about? Why does Julian need to see me?"

Mom didn't have details. She said Julian needed to talk with me. He needed my help with something.

"That's nuts," I said. "I haven't seen Cousin Julian in years. I don't know the guy. There has to be someone else who can help."

Mom didn't say anything, but I thought I could hear her crying softly. The last couple of years since my dad died had been tough on her. "Mom," I said. "Are you okay?"

She sniffled a bit, but then started talking in a steely tone that I barely recognized.

"Jonathan, if you love me, you'll do this. You'll do whatever Julian wants you to do."

"But what. . ." I didn't get a chance to finish my question.

"There will be a plane ticket waiting for you when you get home tonight." She started another sentence, but her voice began to crack. "Jonathan, I need to go," she said and then hung up.

It was hard to concentrate for the rest of the afternoon. The phone call was so unlike my mother—her forcefulness and desperation unnerved me. And then there was the whole mystery of the thing. What on earth did Julian want me to do? I wondered about this life change of his. Had he gone completely off his rocker? Was I going to meet with some old coot ranting about government conspiracies? Some wild-haired fellow who shuffled down the street in his housecoat and slippers? (I knew that's not what mom meant by "crimson robes," but I couldn't get that image out of my mind.) I was so preoccupied by these thoughts that I walked right past Juan's office as I left for the day. It wasn't until I entered the lobby that I realized what I had done. It felt like a bad omen.

When I got back to my apartment, I almost forgot to check the mailbox. I struggled with the bent key for a few minutes, and then the little metal door flew open, spitting pizza flyers and insurance offers all over the floor. As I shoveled them up, my hand settled on a thick envelope. It was from my mother. I sighed, stuffed it in my pocket and headed up the stairs to my apartment.

I opened the envelope while my frozen lasagna entrée spun around in the microwave. Inside was a short note from my mother explaining that Julian was temporarily living in Argentina, and a return airline ticket to Buenos Aires. Good lord, I thought. They want me to take a twelve-hour flight to meet up with a distant cousin for an hour or two? Over the weekend? Great. I would have to spend my entire weekend in a flying sardine tin and disappoint my son. That, or upset my mom even more than she was already disappointed.

I ate my lukewarm lasagna in front of the TV, hoping a large tumbler of Scotch would mask the crumminess of my dinner and the misery of my mood.

I put off phoning Annisha until I was sure Adam would be in bed. Annisha is a stickler for routine, so there was no guess-work there. When she answered the phone she sounded tired, but not unhappy. I braced myself for her mood to change when I told her about my possible weekend plans. But Annisha knew about it already.

"I've talked with your mom, Jonathan," she said. "You need to do this. Adam will understand."

So that was that.

## CHAPTER TWO

THE TAXICAB HAD MOVED from the highway onto an extraordinarily wide boulevard. It looked like a typical city street, lined with trees on either side, a green island separating oncoming traffic, but it was at least ten lanes wide. I had never been to South America before and was surprised by how much Buenos Aires looked like a European city. An enormous obelisk, resembling the Washington Monument, split the scene in front of me, but the buildings and the streets reminded me a little of Paris.

Julian had booked me on a red-eye on Friday night. I had surprised myself by falling asleep on the flight, waking just as the plane was setting down. And now, here it was morning, but in another hemisphere from the one I had fallen asleep in.

The belle époque–style stone buildings, black cast-iron balconies and window boxes continued as we drove, but eventually we moved into an area that looked older, a bit tatty around the edges. There was graffiti on the walls, stucco chipping off the sides of buildings, dusty faded awnings. Although it was a cool fall day here, a number of windows were open, and I could see curtains flapping in the breeze. On one corner, musicians were gathered, playing for a small group of onlookers.

The cab was slowing now, pulling up to a storefront. The sign painted on the window announced tango lessons. Music drifted out of the half-open front door. I double-checked the address Julian had given me. This dance studio appeared to be it. I showed the piece of paper to the cabbie to make sure we were in the right part of town, that this wasn't some sort of mix-up. He nodded and then shrugged his shoulders. I paid and got out of the cab.

*Wow,* I thought, peering through the half-open door. *When Mom said that Julian had changed his life, she wasn't kidding.*

The room was long but not deep. Its walls were painted a rich red, and glass chandeliers hung from the ceiling. Men and women, holding each other closely yet with a certain formality, stepped around the room in time with the pulsing music.

As I watched, a tall, stylishly dressed man separated himself from his partner and threaded his way through the twirling dancers. When he got close to me, I could see he was smiling.

"Jonathan," he said. "I'm so glad you made it." He held out his hand and we shook.

It took me a minute to reconcile the man standing before me with the picture I had imagined on my way here. Julian looked far younger than he had when we met over twenty years ago.

His lean, muscular frame bore no resemblance to the pasty, bloated figure who had sat behind the wheel of that Ferrari. His face was unlined and relaxed. His bright blue eyes seemed to cut right through me.

"Please excuse me," Julian said, waving his hand around the room. "I wasn't sure what time your flight would arrive, so I thought I would take my Saturday lesson. But now that you're here, let's head upstairs."

Julian led me to a door, which I hadn't seen from the entranceway. Opening it, he gestured for me to head up the stairs. When I got to the top, he moved past me and opened another door. "Come in, come in," he said as he stepped into the room.

The apartment was bright and spacious, but nothing like the kind of home I imagined Julian living in. The furniture was an odd assortment of old and new. Posters of musicians and dancers doing the tango adorned the walls, and stacks of books sat on the floor. It looked a bit like the home of a college student.

"I'm sorry to have made you travel such a distance at short notice, but I've been staying in this gorgeous city for the past few months. A friend was looking to sublet his apartment, and since I've always wanted to learn to tango, I thought this was the perfect opportunity. Let me get changed, and then I'll make us some coffee."

Julian disappeared down a long, narrow hallway. I sank into a chair that was covered with a cotton throw with the words "Be Extraordinary" embroidered in its center. I could hear the tango music drifting up the stairs and feel it humming under the floorboards.

As I waited for Julian, my mind began to race. *What was*

*I doing? What did I know of this man?* I felt a powerful sense of unease move through me. Somehow I knew that as soon as Julian walked back into the room, my life would never be the same. I sensed that what lay ahead of me was going to be difficult and exhausting. *I don't have to do this*, I thought. I looked over my shoulder to the doorway, wondering how long it would take me to find another cab. Just then Julian walked back into the room.

He was now wearing a long crimson robe. The hood draped his head.

"Tea or coffee?" he asked as he moved into a small kitchen at the far end of the living room.

"Coffee, please," I said.

I felt awkward sitting in the living room alone; I got up and followed Julian into the kitchen. As Julian prepared the coffee-maker, I looked out of the window, down to the narrow cobble-stoned street. The dance class must have broken up because couples were pouring out onto the sidewalk below. The syncopated music had been replaced with the sound of talking and laughing.

Finally I turned to Julian. "What. . ." I hesitated, trying not to be too indelicate. I started again, "What do you need from me? Why did you want to see me?"

"Jonathan," said Julian, as he leaned against the counter. "Do you know my story?"

I wasn't sure what Julian was getting at. I told him that I knew he had been a litigation lawyer who had made a fortune and had lived a lavish lifestyle. I told him that I heard he'd had a change of heart and left his practice. I wasn't clear about the details.

"It's true," said Julian. "At one point, I was more successful than I had ever dreamed I could be—as far as fame and money go. But I was destroying my life. When I wasn't consumed by work, I was smoking cigars and drinking expensive cognac, having a wild time with young models and new friends. It ruined my marriage, and my lifestyle began to take a toll on my career. I was in a downward spiral, but I didn't know how to stop. One day, in the middle of arguing a big case, I crashed to the floor of the courtroom. A heart attack."

That rang a bell. Mom had probably told me something about this, but I obviously hadn't been paying too much attention.

Julian shook the hood from his head and then reached up to a shelf above the sink to pull down two mugs.

"I spent months recovering my health. During that time, I made a decision."

I sighed. This is where that lovely Ferrari got tossed.

"I sold my mansion, my car, all my possessions. And I headed to India, hoping to learn what I could of the wisdom of the world. You see, building my net worth had become less interesting to me than discovering my self-worth. And chasing beautiful women had given way to pursuing enduring happiness."

I stifled a sigh. It sounded as if this was the beginning of a long story. I was impatient to hear what any of it had to do with me.

"During my travels deep in the Himalayas, I had the great good fortune of coming upon an exceptional man. He was a monk, one of the Sages of Sivana. He took me high into the mountains, to the village where the sages lived, studied and worked. The sages taught me many remarkable lessons that I would love to share with you."

Julian paused and looked down toward my feet. I realized with embarrassment that I had been tapping my foot like some impatient customer in a shop line.

Julian smiled. "But I sense that now is not the time."

"Sorry," I said. "I guess I'm just a little anxious to get back home."

"Not to worry," Julian said gently. "A story should be told only when a listener is ready to hear it."

"You want to know why I asked you here today?" Julian said. I nodded.

The coffee was ready. Julian poured two mugs. "Milk? Sugar?" I shook my head. Julian handed me a mug and then headed into the living room. Once we had both settled in chairs, he continued his story.

"One of the things that the monks taught me was the power of the talismans."

"Talismans?" I said.

"Small statues or amulets. There are nine of them. Each holds a piece of essential wisdom for happiness and a life beautifully lived. Individually, they are just symbolic tokens, but together they hold extraordinary transformative powers. They can, in effect, be lifesaving."

"You need to save a life?" I asked. It sounded a little melodramatic. Or a little crazy.

"Yes. There is someone I know who is in desperate trouble. Others have tried to help, but with no success. This is our last resort."

"Does this have something to do with my mother?" I asked. She had been very upset on the phone.

"It does," said Julian. "But I am not at liberty to explain how."

"Listen, if my mother is sick or something, I have a right to know." I felt my chest get tight, my breathing shallow.

"Your mother is in no danger," said Julian. "That's all I can say."

I was about to press him, to ask more questions, but Julian had drawn his lips together, put his coffee cup down on the table in front of me. It looked as if he was ready to end the conversation. I sighed and looked down at the floor for a minute.

"Okay," I said, "but where do I fit in? What do you need me for?"

Julian had left his chair and moved over to the window. He looked out toward the street below, but his eyes seemed to be focused much farther in the distance.

"When I left the village," Julian said, "the monks gave me the talismans in a leather pouch and asked me to be their new keeper.

"But after I left the Himalayas, I traveled for a while. One night a fire broke out in the small hotel I was staying in. I was out at the time, but my room was destroyed. I was carrying the talismans on me, so the only thing I lost was a pair of sandals. At another inn, I heard a fellow traveler talk of being mugged on a side street in Rome. It occurred to me that while the talismans were being held by the monks in the village, they had been safe. I was the only visitor who had reached that remote place in a very long time. But now that I had these treasures, they were at risk. At any time, they could be stolen, lost or destroyed."

Julian went on to explain that he had decided it would be safer if he sent each talisman to a different trusted safekeeper who would turn it over when Julian had need of it. With each object, he had sent a letter with some descriptions about what he understood the talisman to mean. Now it was clear that he needed these talismans back. He said he wanted me to go and get them.

"What?" I sputtered. "I mean, isn't that what FedEx is for?"

Julian smiled. "I don't think you understand the importance of these talismans. I can't entrust them to a courier or to the mail. They are scattered all over the world, and I need someone I know to pick them up in person."

"And you can't go?" I asked. I knew I was being a little rude, but the image of Julian tangoing across the floor downstairs was still in my mind.

Julian chuckled. "I know that I may not appear to be terribly busy," he said, his tone getting more serious now. "But it is really not possible for me to do this."

I was silent for a few seconds. How could I put this?

"Cousin Julian," I said. "No offense, but you said you need someone you know to pick these things up. You don't *really* know me. I met you once—when I was ten."

"I know you better than you think," said Julian. His pleasant smile had vanished. His eyes were dark, and there was a gravity in his expression that was disconcerting.

"Listen to me, Jonathan," he said quietly. "I can't tell you how I know this, but I do. The *only* person who can collect those talismans is *you.*"

He paused and then added, "I know that my answers aren't very satisfying. But trust me, Jonathan, when I say that this is a matter of life and death."

We sat for a long while in silence. I was thinking about the sound of my mother crying on the phone. The feel of the empty space on Annisha's side of the bed. The look in Adam's eyes when I disappointed him. It isn't very often when you are the "only" one—the only son, the only husband, the only father.

Finally I broke the silence.

"How long will this take?" I asked.

"I've written to all the safekeepers," Julian said. "I haven't heard back from everyone. But I've got a place for you to start—a friend of mine in Istanbul. As far as time goes, well, getting all the talismans will take a few weeks. Maybe a month."

Good lord. That was all my vacation time and then some. I took a deep breath. Julian looked at me and cocked his head.

"Jonathan?" he said.

I looked back at Julian. There was such kindness in his eyes. For a moment, he reminded me of my father, and I realized how much I missed my dad. I also realized that I had made a decision. Words caught in my throat, so I only nodded.

Julian smiled. Then he stood up and ran his hands along the side of his red robe.

"And now," said Julian, "since we have concluded our business, I shall make you some lunch, and then perhaps we should check out the neighborhood. It's called San Telmo. And it's become one of my favorite places on the planet."

I SPENT A PLEASANT, if odd, afternoon with Julian. He took me to a ballroom a few streets away where seasoned tango dancers were giving a show. As the music thumped through my body like a second heartbeat, I noticed Julian's feet tapping, his legs moving slightly as if he were imagining himself doing the moves. Then we walked through the winding alleys until it was time for me to head back for another red-eye flight home. As we stood on the sidewalk outside Julian's apartment, music wafting out of the studio and filling the air around us, Julian turned to me.

"One more thing, Jonathan," he said. From a pocket in his robe, he pulled a small leather-bound notebook. "I'd like you to keep a journal while you are away."

"A diary?" I asked. "What for?"

"Not a diary, Jonathan. A journal. The talismans lend power to those who hold them. But those who have them give these tokens power as well. It is important for me to know your thoughts and feelings about this journey—and about what the talismans mean to you once you are in their presence."

My shoulders slumped. I didn't know what was worse—taking weeks out of my life to travel around the world collecting someone else's stuff, or having to write about it. Self-reflection has never been my forte.

"I think once you are on your own, once you have these incredible talismans in your hands, recording what's in your heart won't be as onerous as it sounds," said Julian.

I was about to say, *sure, whatever,* but I stopped myself. What did it matter? If I was going to do this crazy thing, I might as well do it the way Julian wanted.

Just then the cab pulled up in front of us. As I climbed in, my resolve was nicked by small points of fear. It had been a very long time since I had started something new, begun any sort of adventure. I shut the door and looked back at Julian as the taxi began to edge away from the sidewalk. Julian raised his hand to wave, and then called out to me.

"Jonathan," he said, "be joyful. It's not every day that you get to save a life!"

IT TOOK ALL MY NERVE to get in my car on Monday morning and head into the office. I had three weeks of vacation coming, and I would have to take them as soon as possible. But if the journey took longer than that, I could be in real trouble. All I could ask for was unpaid time off, and if the answer was no, I guess I was out of a job.

But honestly, I said to myself, as I hauled my reluctant carcass out of the car and forced myself through the front doors of the office, what did one foolish choice matter? After all, in the past, I had always made what I thought were great decisions at the time. And where had that got me? My job had become a constant source of stress and frustration. My wonderful wife was leaving me. Whatever savings I had built up through all my hard work were going to be decimated by divorce. And even the joy I felt with Adam was being eaten away by the guilt I had, seeing him only on the weekends—and being such a lousy dad even then. Could one crazy move like this trip really cause me any more pain than all my sensible decisions had brought me?

I spent an hour swiveling in my desk chair, wallowing in disappointment and pessimism. By the time I walked into my boss's office, I had accepted my whole predicament with fatalistic resignation. I had, in fact, almost forgotten how difficult this discussion was going to be.

I was quickly reminded, however, once the first few sentences had left my mouth.

I had settled into one of the strategically low office chairs that faced David's mammoth desk. He had hardly looked up from his computer as I walked in. But as I explained that I needed to take my vacation, and perhaps even more time to deal with a family emergency overseas, he raised his head. His expression could only be described as "stunned." As I launched into an explanation about my accumulated vacation days, he held up his hand.

"Let me get this straight," David said. "You want twenty-one days off in a row, without notice?"

I couldn't help myself. "Well, technically, Saturday and Sunday are called 'the weekend,' so no, not twenty-one straight days."

"Jonathan, you know damn well that no one is allowed to take more than two weeks' vacation in a row," he shot back.

The conversation only got worse when I said that I didn't know exactly when I would return.

"Of all the people in this organization," David said, "you're the last person I would have thought would pull a stunt like this."

"I know," I said. He was right.

"You know, Jonathan, you're considered a rising star around here. And before today, if you asked me to name one person who was going to come out of this sale or merger or whatever it is looking like the golden boy, I would have said it was you. But you take off like this, at this time. . ."

He turned to look at the window. He was twirling a pen between his fingers, a frown stiffening his face.

I didn't need to hear this.

"Look," I said. "I talked to Nawang over the weekend. She has agreed to manage my projects during my absence. She knows what she's doing. And she can always try me on my phone in an emergency. So—can I take my vacation, or do I have to resign?"

"Take the vacation," David said tersely. "But I'll tell you one thing. If we can do without you for a month, we can probably do without you forever."

I got up from the chair and headed for the door. Before I crossed the threshold, I stopped and turned.

"David, would you have said the same thing if I'd made this request because something was going on with my wife or son?"

David continued to stare out the window. His expression was unreadable.

The walk back to my office was a long one. It was chilling to think that David might not care about helping me if my child was ill or in need. But why did I expect anything different? This place did things to people. I had seen that with Juan.

Juan. There wasn't a day I didn't think about my old boss, my old friend. As the months passed, I had found it increasingly difficult not to be distracted by his absence. I often found myself waking up in the night, unable to fall back to sleep, going over and over events in my mind, reliving my part in the whole disaster. But no matter how often I replayed it, I couldn't put it behind me. Getting away from it all was probably the best thing I could do.

THE NEXT FEW DAYS were a maelstrom. I scrambled to resolve things at work. I let loose a tsunami of messages and phone calls. I blew around town, doing banking, picking up dry cleaning, attempting drive-by visits with my son. Even packing was chaotic—how did I know what to take if I didn't even know all the places I would be heading to?

And then I was sitting on the red-eye flight. To Turkey. On my way to meet a friend of Julian's. My phone was turned off; there was no paperwork in my overhead luggage. I had many quiet hours by myself with nothing I had to do, nothing I *could* do. I was hoping to rest, but my mind was still racing. I took out a piece of paper from my jacket pocket. Julian had sent me a brief note with the airline tickets.

"Thank you," it said, "for taking time away from your family and your work to take this voyage. I know you had a dozen reasons not to go, but one of the best gifts we can give ourselves is to get rid of our excuses. Rudyard Kipling once wrote, 'We have forty million reasons for failure, but not a single excuse.' And the dangerous thing about excuses is that if we recite them enough times, we actually come to believe they are true. This task I've asked you to do involves a lot of travel, but I hope that you can focus on the opportunities it provides rather than the inconveniences it may pose. Life itself is a journey after all, and what matters most is not what you are getting, but who you are becoming."

Julian had also sent a small leather pouch on a long cord. I was supposed to wear it around my neck and put the talismans in it as I collected them. For now, it was in my jacket pocket. I fingered the soft leather absentmindedly.

Everyone around me on the plane was falling asleep. There was a gentle hum of the engines; the subtle rattle of the drinks cart disappearing to the back. I closed my eyes. I thought about Annisha and Adam. Somehow I knew, being so far away, I would miss them all the more. Then I thought about the other people missing from my life. My dad's absence was a dull ache that was lodged in my chest. But it was pain with a certain gentleness, accompanied as it was by so many happy memories. Then there was Juan. Julian's words came back to me. "It's not every day you get to save a life."

Wasn't that the truth?

## CHAPTER THREE

JULIAN HAD NOT GIVEN ME a list of the places I would be going or the names of the safekeepers I would meet. "Different locations" was all he would reveal in Buenos Aires. "Europe, Asia, North America. I haven't managed to contact everyone yet," he had said. I would start, however, in Istanbul, where I would meet his old friend Ahmet Demir.

"Ahmet will meet you at the airport. I know he'll want to show you a little of his wonderful city, but, I'm sorry, you won't have much time to play tourist. You're booked to fly to Paris the following day."

Play tourist! That made me laugh. I just wanted to get these talisman things as quickly as possible and get back to work. Even as I stumbled off the plane at the Atatürk airport, I was snapping on my phone, checking for messages from Nawang, thinking about what might be happening in my absence at the office. There were a number from people asking me how long I would be gone. A message from my mother was chipper and evasive. I had asked her if she knew anything more about who Julian was trying to help with these talismans, but she was claiming to be unsure. I didn't believe her—I had heard the emotion in her voice.

The messages on my phone kept me distracted as I made my way through the long passport line and the baggage claim. So when I finally stood at the arrivals exit with my suitcase in hand, it was the first time I had wondered how I might recognize this Ahmet fellow—how we were expected to find each other in the crowd.

As I scanned the gathering of family members, drivers and other eager people clustered in the arrivals lobby, I spotted a tall man holding up a sign with my name on it. He had silver hair, a short gray beard and a warm grin. I gave him a little wave and headed over.

When I got close, Ahmet dropped his sign and took my outstretched hand in his, pumping it vigorously. "*Hoş geldiniz, hoş geldiniz,*" he said. "A pleasure to meet a member of Julian's family. I am honored."

I muttered something inadequate in reply, overwhelmed by Ahmet's enthusiasm.

"You have everything?" asked Ahmet. "Are you ready to go?" I nodded, and Ahmet picked up the sign, placed his hand gently on my elbow and guided me out of the terminal.

Ahmet led me through the crowded car park and stopped in front of a shiny silver Renault. "Here we are," he announced, taking my bag and popping the trunk. I opened the passenger door and was just sliding across the seat when my phone started to beep. "Excuse me," I said to Ahmet. I buckled my seat belt and started to read.

A message from Nawang said that she had received a call from one of my clients. An alarming number of complaints had come in from the man's dealers about a new component we had designed for their most popular sedan model. I had a sick feeling in the pit of my stomach. This was the kind of thing that could lead to a recall, if not some kind of financial claim against us. Nawang would need to get the quality control department started on testing to get to the bottom of the problem.

"I'm sorry," I said to Ahmet as he pulled out of the parking lot. "I just have to send out a few messages. Work emergency." Ahmet nodded kindly. "Do what you have to do," he said. "We will get acquainted soon enough."

The car hurtled along, although I saw nothing of the world we moved through. My eyes were glued to the screen of my phone. I was vaguely aware of a congested highway and speeding traffic, then of moving across a bridge over water. But by the time I really looked up, we were weaving in and out of narrow streets, the car clearly headed up a steady incline.

Ahmet seemed to notice that he had me back.

"I thought that after your long flight you may want to clean up a bit before we head out again. I am taking you to my apartment in Beyoğlu."

We were moving slowly now, past cafés and shops, narrow sidewalks filled with pedestrians, low-rise buildings of gray and yellow stone and brick. Ahead I could see a tower rising at the top of the hill, a blue-gray peak pointing into the sky, with two rows of windows below. There were people moving around a walkway outside the upper set of windows.

"The Galata Tower," said Ahmet. "Stunning views of the city from there."

Ahmet slowed and pulled the car into a small space on the street.

"Here we are," he said, pointing to the three-story building next to us. Out on the sidewalk, Ahmet opened the heavy wooden door of the building and ushered me in. There was a set of marble stairs in front of us.

"You don't mind climbing, do you?" said Ahmet.

"Not at all," I replied.

AHMET'S APARTMENT WAS beautifully furnished, the floors covered with elegantly patterned carpets, the brocade sofa adorned with brightly colored pillows, the walls tastefully appointed with framed pictures of seabirds and boats, flora and fauna. But it seemed curiously impersonal. Julian had told me that Ahmet was a ferry captain. I had imagined him living in more rustic quarters.

"As you may have guessed, I don't spend much time here," said Ahmet. "I bought this apartment several years ago, as an investment. Usually it is rented out to foreigners who work in the embassies or businesses in this part of the city. But my wife died a few years ago, and I recently sold our family home in Beşiktaş. So I use this place when I am ferrying the boat or showing people around the old city. The rest of the time, I spend in the village where I grew up, just up the Bosphorus."

"Come," said Ahmet, walking over to the windows. "Let me show you."

I hadn't appreciated how high up we had climbed in the car,

or where Ahmet's building was located, but as I gazed out the living room windows, I became immediately aware of how wonderful his investment had been. Stretched in front of me was the breadth of one of the most amazing sights I have ever seen.

"There," said Ahmet, pointing to the river below us. "That river, that is the Golden Horn. There's the Atatürk Bridge and the Galata Bridge. My little boat is docked in that harbor there. And to your left, that great body of water is the Bosphorus Strait. My city continues on the other side of it. But here you stand in Europe. Once on the other side of Istanbul, you stand in Asia."

I looked across to the Asian continent, but then back to the skyline directly in front of me.

"Ah, yes," said Ahmet. "That is something, isn't it? The old city. Sultanahmet. The Bazaar Quarter. Seraglio Point."

I could see in the distance two enormous complexes with domed roofs and minarets, gardens and walls.

"Hagia Sophia?" I asked. It was the only thing I really knew about Istanbul. The great domed church built by Emperor Justinian when this place was Constantinople, the seat of the Roman Empire, the adoptive home of the Christian Church. It had been converted later into a mosque, the minarets added and the interior modified, but the original mosaics remained. Still stunningly beautiful I had heard.

"The one just to the left," said Ahmet, pointing. "The Blue Mosque behind her. And the Hippodrome, Topkapi Palace, the Cistern, museums—so much to see." Ahmet swept his hand back and forth across the vista in front of us. "But this afternoon, I will take you to the Spice Bazaar and the Grand Bazaar before we head for the boat."

"The boat?"

"Ah, yes," replied Ahmet, moving away from the window. "I'm sorry. I don't have the talisman here. It is at my village home, in Anadolu Kavaği."

I had forgotten all about the reason for my visit.

"We could drive, but what's the point, really?" Ahmet continued. "A boat is the best way to get there. My son has the boat out this morning for a private tour, so we will go tonight and come back tomorrow morning." Ahmet was gesturing for me to follow him. "Now I will show you where you can clean up. Then we will have tea and lunch before we head out to the bazaar."


THE FIRST THING that hit me when we walked into the Spice Bazaar was the fragrance. It was like walking through some sort of aromatic garden, the scents shifting with every step we took, mingling, each overtaking the next.

Stalls followed one after another. There were mounds of dates and other dried fruits, all sorts of nuts, great pyramids of softly colored halvah. There were cylinders of nougat and torrone, and an astonishing assortment of jewel-colored Turkish delight—*lokum,* Ahmet told me it was called here.

Counters were filled with open boxes of tea. Small hills of ground spices spilled from the front, stall after stall—turmeric, cumin, cardamom, paprika, nutmeg, cinnamon.

Ahmet bought some dried apricots, dates and figs before we left and made our way to the enormous stone complex that housed the thousands of shops of the Grand Bazaar.

The Spice Bazaar had dazzled my senses, stupefying me with its exotic aromas. I had been moving about utterly absorbed by my surroundings, not thinking at all about myself or my life. But here, in the Grand Bazaar, my mind kept jumping to the people I missed. As I walked through the huge, endless arched corridors, I saw so many things that Annisha might like—mosaic lamps, delicate silk scarves, intricately patterned ceramics—and everywhere a riot of color. That was one thing that had struck me when I first met Annisha. No matter what she wore, there was always a splash of vibrant color somewhere on her—bright green earrings, a purple scarf in winter, a brilliant orange beret. Her apartment was like that, too—an eclectic assortment of things, a jumble of pattern and hues, chaotic yet surprisingly harmonious. Of course I would be traveling for the next few weeks, so I couldn't buy anything bulky. And I was overwhelmed by the choices. Eventually I picked out a *nazar* necklace for her—the glass "evil eye" bead is believed by many to ward off harm—and for Adam I bought a little embroidered vest that I thought he'd get a kick out of.

The carpet sellers most distracted me. They called out each time I passed, and each time I found myself slowly looking over the beautiful carpets.

Ahmet noticed my attention. "Ah, yes," he said. "You must come back someday when you have more time, when you can really shop and bargain. Choosing a good carpet is not easy—you must learn about the art, the weaving and knotting, the fiber, the dyes. But you must also learn how to value them—and how to bargain for them. I would love to instruct you in this."

Ahmet's eagerness to teach me reminded me of my parents. They were a dynamic duo who encouraged lifelong learning. Mom was a voracious reader, and when my sister and I were in elementary school, she took a job at a small bookstore. She came home with so many books that I'm sure the store kept her employed so they wouldn't lose their best customer. She bought fiction for herself, nonfiction for my dad, and picture books and early readers for Kira and me.

Dad was delighted with this development, and he devoured the reading material with glee. But Dad's enthusiasm didn't stop there. Nothing gave Nick Landry more pleasure than *sharing* his knowledge. He was, in fact, an elementary school teacher, but teaching was more than his job—it was his passion. Between the two of them, my parents created a classroom atmosphere wherever we went—much to the consternation of their children.

Every year, we took one family trip during the summer holidays. It was never anywhere exotic, but Mom and Dad always did their research before we got there. Hiking through the woods, Mom would pull a field guide from her knapsack and tell us how Jack pines actually needed the intense heat of forest fire to open their cones so they could seed themselves. Then Dad would explain how a beaver constructed its dam, or how the hills we climbed were once the shores of ancient lakes. At any historical site, Mom and Dad knew more about the place than the guides. Even a theme park could be a lesson in centrifugal force or pop culture references.

Mom and Dad seemed almost addicted to information and ideas, and our travels were always punctuated with exclamations. "Isn't that something!" Mom would say anytime we made a discovery. And Dad loved it when my sister and I showed curiosity. "Great question!" he would blurt out with joy and pride when we asked anything at all. You would have thought we had just discovered a cure for cancer.

These days I remember that enthusiasm with fondness, but as a child I often wearied of it. And when I hit my teens, our little excursions, the constant instruction, the endless trivia were like nails on a blackboard. Slumped in the backseat of a hot car on a summer afternoon, while Dad gave us a heartfelt account of the Erie Canal, Kira and I would roll our eyes, raise our index fingers to our temples and fire imaginary guns.

This place, this city, I thought sadly, would have fascinated my parents. This was the kind of trip they always dreamed about, the kind of place they hoped to visit. That was their big plan for their retirement: travel. In fact, when Dad left work, his colleagues presented him with a set of luggage. In the months following their retirement, travel books sprouted up around the house like mushrooms on a wet lawn. Stacks piled up beside his favorite living room chair, volumes spilling out from under his bedside table, brochures and maps peeking out of the magazine rack in the bathroom—Ireland, Tuscany, Thailand, New Zealand. Dad printed off itineraries and posted them above his computer desk. He and Mom were planning to be on the road for almost half a year.

Then one day, several months before their planned departure, Mom heard a crash from the garage. Dad was putting away the patio furniture for the winter when an aortic embolism struck. He was dead before he even touched the floor.

For months after the funeral, Mom moved as if under water. Slowly the itineraries disappeared from the bulletin board, the travel books were moved to a shelf in the basement, and Mom went back to her part-time job at the bookstore. Kira thought Mom might return to thoughts of travel someday, but right now, she still couldn't bear to think about it without Dad.

One last shout from a carpet seller interrupted my thoughts about my parents. Ahmet began heading out of the bazaar into the late afternoon sunshine.

"Time for dinner," Ahmet said as ushered me around the side of the building. We turned down one alley, then another, winding our way through the narrow streets of the old city. Eventually Ahmet stopped in front of a bright red awning that stretched out from a low stone building.

"Here we are," he said. I followed him into the shade. The café was dim and cool, but brimming with color. Red and gold rugs hung from the stone wall, and underneath them were low benches lined with huge blue and orange pillows. Small, squat tables, covered in bright red-striped cloth, sat in front of the benches. A little brass lamp adorned each table.

Over a dinner of peppers stuffed with rice and pine nuts, lamb with pureed eggplant, and sesame-seed bread, Ahmet and I talked about our work and our lives. More than once, however, friendly silences fell over the table. The quiet might be punctuated by "Try this," from Ahmet, or "That was good," from me, but there were long stretches when we let the distant sound of voices from the street take over. I felt far away from everything I had ever known.

The sun was just beginning to lower in the sky when we arrived at the dock. The tang of salt water spiced the air. The harbor was crammed with boats large and small, huge commercial ferries dominating the space. Ahmet, I learned, was not just a ferry captain. He had actually owned one of these big ferry companies, but sold it a number of years ago. He was now semiretired. He had kept only one boat from the fleet—a vessel that originally was a fishing boat and had served as the first ferry in the early days of his business. "I could not bear to part with it," he told me. "I take it out now and then for private trips up the Bosphorus. I had already booked one for today when Julian called. So my son took it out for me."

We walked past the docks where the large public ferries waited, and past the large tourist boats. Alongside one of the docks was a long, shallow craft with ornate bow and stern decorations, an elaborate canopy and gunwales shining with gold gilt. "A replica of an imperial caïque," said Ahmet. "For tourists."

Eventually we arrived at an area where the slips held smaller vessels. Ahmet walked up to a modest white boat with blue trim. "Here it is," he said, laughing. "My pride and joy." It was a sturdy-looking tug-like boat. Near the prow was a small open-topped wheel house, and behind a small wood-and-glass partition were the control panel and wheel. A worn leather stool was placed behind the wheel. Wooden benches lined the stern, and a few seats ran behind the wheel house. The white and blue paint of the sides and floor was cracked, but clean. Old, but well cared for.

"It seems we have missed Yusuf. Oh well. Perhaps on your next visit I will be able to introduce you to my family," said Ahmet as he untied the boat from the dock.

It did not take long for us to get out of the harbor into the open strait. We were moving slowly, but at this time of night it seemed as if everything was operating at such a leisurely speed. A large ferry with its lights twinkling churned toward the Asian shore, and smaller boats were off in the distance. The water felt unnaturally quiet. In the twilight I could see Istanbul stretching out from both shores—an elaborate quilt of mosques, palaces and other elegant buildings, interspersed with red-tiled roofs, apartment houses, palm trees, shops and cafés. We slipped under the Bosphorus Bridge and headed north. I could make out elaborate wooden houses, what Ahmet told me were *yalis*—summer homes of the rich—hanging over the water's edge as if they were floating instead of anchored onshore. With every passing minute, the sky became a deeper blue, until the full moon looked like a giant pearl hanging before an inky pool. Its light bounced against the water, and Ahmet slowed the engine even further. I could feel the boat bob against the gentle rhythm of the current.

"It is special here, no?" said Ahmet. I nodded.

"It doesn't seem quite real," I said.

"But it's so hard to say what is real, isn't it?" Ahmet went on.

"I suppose." This wasn't the kind of thing I usually spent much time thinking about.

I walked to the stern of the boat and looked back at the disappearing city.

"Did you know," continued Ahmet, "that a strait is not like a river? Water does not flow in one direction only."

I turned around to look at Ahmet and shook my head.

"No," said Ahmet. "Not like a river at all. Water is pulled in and out by ocean tides. Just as Europe is meeting Asia here, at this spot, the waters of two seas, the Marmara and the Black Sea, are coming together, mingling. And yet, even this is not exactly what it seems."

"What do you mean?" I asked.

"There were marine scientists from England, Canada and Turkey studying this strait a few years ago," Ahmet explained. "And you know what they discovered?" Ahmet had been facing ahead as he steered, but now he looked over his shoulder at me. I shrugged my shoulders and shook my head.

"At the very bottom of this strait, there runs an undersea river. Water, mud and sediment, heavier than the salt water above, flowing from the Marmara Sea into the Black Sea."

"An underwater river?" I said. "How bizarre."

"It makes you realize," said Ahmet, "just how complicated things are. How things are seldom simply what they appear to be."

I had moved around the boat and now joined Ahmet in a seat next to the wheel. We were both silent for several minutes. Then Ahmet tilted back in his seat.

"We have spent the better part of the day together," Ahmet said thoughtfully. "But in truth we don't know much of each other. Of my dear friend Julian's relative, I know only this: you are an electrical engineer; you are married; you have a six-year-old son. But who are you really?"

I didn't have an answer for that. Ahmet glanced at my blank expression and smiled.

"And it is no different with me," he said. "I told you at dinner that I am a sixty-year-old business owner. That I am a widower with four grown sons. But do you really know me?"

"It is a place to start, I suppose," I answered. "I mean, I could ask you more about your company or your sons."

"But it would take us a long time to truly get to know one another, wouldn't it?"

"Yes, I guess so."

"That's the way it usually is. But just imagine if we started our conversations with other things. What if I told you that for me life is on the water. Ever since I was a child, all I wanted to do was live and work on or near the water? My mother used to tell me that the only time I was really content as a baby was when she gave me a bath. Water, fishing, swimming. Boats, boats, boats. No doubt about what I wanted to do. When I am not on one of my boats, I always feel a strange sense of restlessness. Sometimes that was hard for my wife, for my sons, to deal with. But our best times were always together, on the seashore or on the boat. It's as if that was where we could all be ourselves. I have always needed to be on the water—to think, to really understand the world and my life. It was on this same little boat that I decided that Kaniz was the woman I wanted to marry. It was here where I have made all my plans and all my biggest decisions." Ahmet turned the wheel of the boat slightly. "I feel if told you *that,* you might really begin to understand me."

"I guess most of what we understand about people is just the surface stuff," I offered.

"Yes," said Ahmet, nodding. "And that is a sad thing." Ahmet was silent for a moment.

"But that is not the saddest thing," he continued reflectively. "The saddest thing is that this is often all we understand about ourselves: that so often, we live our neighbor's life, instead of our own."

It was hard to tell how long we were actually on the Bosphorus. The phosphorescent water, the shimmering moon, the soothing hum of the engine made the journey seem like a dream, a moment out of time. But then Ahmet was turning the wheel and pointing at distant lights dotting the shore on the Asian side.

"Anadolu Kavaği," Ahmet said pointing ahead. You cannot see it, but up there, on the hill, are the ruins of the Genoese Castle. From the fourteenth century. My little house is the other way, at the southern end of the village, along the shore."

It didn't take us long to dock the boat and then drive the little car that Ahmet had parked at the docks to his home in the village. The small stone house was nothing like the apartment that Ahmet kept in the city. Terra cotta tiles lined the floors, uneven plaster covered the walls, and the dark, rough timbers of the ceiling seemed to hold echoes from a distant past. Open shelves in the kitchen were lined with heavy crockery and brass cookware. Here and there were small bits of mosaic and brightly colored glass, but the woven window coverings and faded spreads on the furniture had the muted shades of time. Ahmet carried my backpack into a tiny room. He pointed to the small bed, no larger than a twin, its hand-carved frame pushed against the wall.

"The bed in which I slept with my two brothers," Ahmet laughed. He put my knapsack at the foot of the bed, and then led me back to the living room. "Shall we sit outside for just a bit?" he asked.

We put on sweaters and moved out to the little stone patio overlooking the moonlit Bosphorus. Ahmet told me more about his favorite place, the water.

"It is said that the Black Sea used to be a freshwater lake. Thousands and thousands of years ago, there was an enormous flood, the Mediterranean spilled into the Bosphorus Strait here and turned the Black Sea into a saltwater ocean."

"And the undersea river—do you think it might be a remnant of that?" I asked him.

"That's what it sounds like, doesn't it?" said Ahmet. "You know, some people think that the flood was the one that the Bible talks about—Noah's flood."

"No kidding," I said.

"And the Bosphorus figures in Greek mythology as well. Are you familiar with Jason—of the Golden Fleece?"

I shook my head.

"Well, in Greek mythology, the Bosphorus was the home of the Symplegades—floating rock cliffs that would clash together and crush boats that dared make passage here. When Jason sailed down the Bosphorus, he sent a dove to fly between the rocks. The rocks crashed together, but the dove lost only its tail feathers. Then Jason and the Argonauts followed. The stern of their ship was clipped, but the boat did not founder. After Jason's passage, the rocks stopped moving and the Greeks finally had access to the Black Sea."

I smiled and nodded. My mom would have loved Ahmet and his stories.

"Oh dear," said my host. "I had almost forgotten why you were here. Julian's talisman. Let me get that for you." Ahmet stood up quickly and entered the house. He returned a few minutes later with a small square of folded paper and a little bundle of red silk. He handed both to me.

"Well, now that you have what you came for," he said, "we should go to bed. Tomorrow we will get up early. Head back to Istanbul. I can take you to Ayasofya—Hagia Sophia—before we make our way to the airport. But you will have to promise me to return someday so I can show you the rest of my home."

I agreed happily and reluctantly rose from my chair.

WHEN I GOT BACK into the room, I placed the small bundle on a little round table next to the bed. I sat on the edge of the bed for a minute before I picked up the parcel again. Slowly

I unfolded the soft square of silk. There in the middle was a small brass coin. Well, not a coin exactly. It was a disk, about the size of a nickel. On one side was stamped a sun, its rays radiating from a raised circle. On the other side, a crescent moon. I put the coin on the table and picked up the piece of folded parchment. I opened it and placed it on my knees. I read:

*The Power of Authenticity*

*The most important gift we can give ourselves is the commit-ment to living our authentic life. To be true to ourselves, however, is not an easy task. We must break free of the seductions of society and live life on our own terms, under our own values and aligned with our original dreams. We must tap our hidden selves; explore the deep-seated, unseen hopes, desires, strengths and weaknesses that make us who we are. We have to understand where we have been and know where we are going. Every decision we make, every step we take, must be informed by our commitment to living a life that is true and honest and authentic to ourselves and ourselves alone. And as we proceed, we are certain to experience fortune well beyond our highest imagination.*

I went to my backpack, and from the bottom I dug out the journal that Julian had given me. Then I slipped the parchment between its covers and put the journal back inside. I picked up the talisman again and turned it back and forth in my hands. Then I took the little leather pouch from my pocket and slipped the disk inside before turning back the covers on the bed and crawling in.

I WOKE THE NEXT MORNING, realizing that I had not moved a muscle all night. It was the kind of deep sleep I enjoyed only on vacation. When I padded into the kitchen, the wonderful aroma of Turkish coffee, pungent and dark, filled my nostrils. Ahmet served rich yogurt and fruit with the coffee, and then hustled me out the door, back through the cobbled village streets and to the water once more.

After we climbed into the boat, Ahmet started the engine and carefully backed away from the dock. Once the boat was out in the open water, he accelerated. We were moving faster than we had the night before, but that wasn't the only thing that was utterly changed.

Despite the early hour, the sun was blazing in the sky. The villages, the green hills, the water—everything seemed bright and clear, sharp and vibrant. It was stunning, but the myth and mysteries of the previous night had evaporated. "It all looks so different," I said to Ahmet. "Beautiful, but different."

"Yes," said Ahmet thoughtfully. "I often find that myself. Night hides many things, but reveals others."

"It happens in cities, too," I said. "Some often look magical at night but humdrum during the day."

"And yet both versions are equally real." Ahmet paused, and then added, "I suppose that is why it is never a good idea to make quick judgments about things. It takes a long time to really get to know places, people, even ourselves."

The boat was humming through the water as birds circled and swung above us. Up ahead I could see two men throw a net from a small fishing boat. A young boy broke away from a group of people gathered on a dock and waved vigorously at us. I felt for a moment that I had traveled along these shores before but was only noticing them for the first time.

"Yes," I said to my new friend Ahmet. "Yes, I am beginning to see the truth in that."

# Chapter Four

THERE HAD BEEN MOMENTS WHEN, moving around Istanbul, I felt as if I were a character in a movie. As if I were seeing the world through a camera, as if every word that came out of my mouth had been written by someone else. It was disorienting, but at the same time refreshing, as if the world was full of possibility. The night I'd floated down the Bosphorus, with the moon above, the water below—I don't think I'd felt that sense of wonder since I was a child. Julian had said that life was about "becoming." I was beginning to feel that.

But here, sitting in the Atatürk airport, *that* Istanbul was slipping quickly into the rearview mirror. I had shut off my phone previous afternoon and, until now, had forgotten to turn it on. It hummed awake, producing an inbox stuffed with semi-hysterical subject lines: "Urgent shipping request"; "QC question"; "XD95 failure"; "Monthly account reports due!"; "Where the Hell R U?" I noticed several texts from Nawang, and I read through those first. It sounded as if the first quality control tests were going well. Then I tackled the ones from David. Just requests for reports I'd already given him, information I had already shared. How much of my time did I waste resending stuff, repeating myself, churning out documents and messages no one ever bothered to read (but were nevertheless due—and submitted—on time, each month, each week)? Forty minutes clicked by before I turned to the messages from Annisha and Adam. Annisha wanted to know if I had arrived in Istanbul safely. Damn. I should have let her know as soon as I had arrived. Adam wanted to tell me about his school play. I quickly typed replies and then called the office, hoping I could catch Nawang.

BY THE TIME I was herded into my seat on the plane, I was thoroughly back in *my* world. I couldn't keep ignoring my work, my life, every time I landed in a new place. And if my inbox wasn't full the next time I turned on my phone, what would that mean? It couldn't be a good thing. I pulled a few items from my carry-on and then wrestled it into the overhead bin. I could hear the fellow behind me huffing and puffing. A baby was already wailing at the back of the plane. I gritted my teeth and sighed. As I struggled into the kindergarten-sized seats that pass as airline accommodation these days, I could feel the muscles in my neck tightening up. The leather pouch that Julian had given me for the talismans was on a long leather cord. I had put it around my neck, figuring I was less likely to lose it this way. But now I could feel the leather string digging into my skin. The pouch felt unnaturally heavy. Too heavy for the tiny amulet it contained. I clicked my seat belt in place, then took the pouch from under my shirt. I pulled out the little coin and turned it back and forth. The sun and the moon. Yin and yang. Heart and head. Heaven and Earth. Hidden and revealed. I put it in the pouch and dropped the leather bag back under my shirt.

Then I pulled the journal from my jacket pocket. Julian's note about authenticity was inside. I hadn't really thought about it since I first read it. In Istanbul, I felt as if I wasn't really living my life. Or maybe it was more like standing outside my life, looking at it as a stranger might. Now I wondered if what I saw was real. What was my "authentic" self? Who was I, really? I remembered my conversation with Ahmet on the boat. I had told him I was an electrical engineer. A husband. A father. All those things were true, but they could apply to thousands of other men. How would I describe myself if I couldn't rely on those three labels?

I pulled down the tray table and laid the notebook open on top of it. As I've said, I have never been the kind of person who spends a great deal of time on self-reflection. Mostly, I just couldn't see the point.

I took a pen from my pocket and, at the top of the first page, wrote, "Who am I?" I felt foolish.

I stared at the blank page until the flight attendant broke my trance by offering me a beverage. She served me with a bright smile and then continued down the aisle. I took a sip of coffee and was about to snap the notebook shut, but stopped myself. This was ridiculous. I should be able to answer the question I had posed.

But even after I had finished my coffee, I was staring at a blank page. The flight was almost four hours long. I had promised myself I would write something before it was over. Maybe if I couldn't describe my "authentic" self, I could think about times in my life when I felt I really knew who I was, when I felt aware of my life, when I felt I was living just as I wanted to rather than how everyone around me suggested I live.

The first thing I wrote was "story time." It seemed like a strange moment to highlight because it wasn't a single moment or even a single time. And it was so, so long ago. During all the years of my childhood, we had a family ritual. Once dinner and baths were out of the way, my mother would take my sister and me into one of our bedrooms. The three of us would climb into bed, and Mom would begin to read. When I was tiny it was picture books. Later it was short novels, and then, eventually, long tomes, like *Kidnapped* or *Gulliver's Travels*. We kept that up longer than I would ever have admitted to any of my friends. There was something about those times as a child, however, that acted as a touchstone for me. No matter what had happened during the day, what trouble I had got into, what fights Kira and I had had, what disasters had befallen me at school—in that hour on the bed at night, my mother's soft voice reverberating in the air, the sound of Dad downstairs banging around the kitchen as he cleaned up, my sister's contented breathing filling in the spaces—everything fell into place. I knew who I was and where I belonged.

Next I wrote about a more specific memory. "Hiking with Annisha in the Rockies," I put down. That was just before we got married. Climbing the Grassi Lake trail outside of Canmore, a town in western Canada, we had crossed a small creek.

Annisha was following me; I reached out to help her across. When we got to the top of the trail we gazed at the landscape surrounding us, the mountains that encircled us. Then I looked at Annisha. I remember so clearly that I was overcome with the feeling that this improbable place was exactly where I wanted to be, exactly where I *should be* at this moment.

Of course, back then I couldn't imagine the feeling that overcame me when Adam was born. That was my third point. I remember thinking, while holding him as Annisha dozed in the hospital bed, that my place in the universe was forever defined by this small baby. I was a father. And I always would be. There was a certainty about it that was sobering and yet comforting.

And finally I wrote, "Fuel-injection design trial run." It seemed like an oddly technical, professional event to follow Adam's birth, but there it was. The first independent project I had completed at work. Juan had asked me to take a crack at a new fuel-injection system. "Don't just tinker with the previous designs," he said. "You've talked to me about doing things differently. So do it. Start from scratch. Rethink the whole thing."

I worked for months on that design. But it hardly felt like that. I would sit down at my desk in the morning and barely move until it was six p.m. I would get out of my car in the evening, stand in the driveway and wonder how I got there. I was so consumed with ideas, overcome with energy. I got up in the mornings itching to get to the office.

When I eventually presented my drawings and schematics to Juan, he looked thoughtful. "Well," he told me. "There's really only one way we can find out if this will work. Let's build it."

So we did. Then we ran it. Eventually we put it into a vehicle. And we drove that car. I didn't sleep at all the night before.

Watching the car speed around the test track, I could almost hear my heart ringing, like a chiming clock.

Four things. That was enough for one day. I closed the book and shoved it into my pocket. I leaned my seat back as far as it would go, closed my eyes and tried to sleep.

As soon as I got into the terminal at Charles de Gaulle Airport, my pulse started to race. The lineup at customs seemed interminable, the wait for my bag an eternity. When I burst through the glass doors in front of the cab stand, I sped to the first taxi like a kid running for an ice cream truck. I love Paris, and I was eager to start walking its streets.

But the cab ride into the city was slow. It was about six p.m., the expressway thick with traffic. Unlike my time in Istanbul, this felt oddly familiar. I was surrounded by commuters: drivers watching the road with only half-hearted attention, their minds congested with thoughts of their day—what they had accomplished and what they would face tomorrow. That should have been me, only on the other side of the globe. Instead, here I was, a passenger, chugging through a landscape that was familiar yet foreign, the wall of gray suburban high-rises lining the highway reminding me that, in a city of millions, I knew no one.

Julian had told me that I would be staying at a hotel on the Champs Élysées. But I didn't want to get out of the cab when it pulled in front. I almost told the driver to keep going. Nothing appealed to me more at that moment than the thought of driving through the Paris streets until the sun set—the lights of the Eiffel Tower twinkling in the background everywhere we went.

Julian, however, had said that I would be meeting with a man named Antoine Gaucher, but he couldn't tell me exactly when. Antoine, he said, would leave a letter for me at the desk, telling me where to meet him—and I supposed that Antoine could be waiting for me even now. After all, Julian had said, "Antoine is an interesting individual. It may be an unusual meeting."

As the cab drove away, down the Champs Élysées, I pushed myself through the doors of the hotel. The lobby was crowded. Dozens of people in business clothes, their name tags around their necks, lined up in front of the reception desk, with more of the group gathered in clusters throughout the lobby. Near the concierge's desk, a small girl sat on top of a suitcase, sobbing. A haggard-looking woman stood over her, digging in her purse for something. The lobby was reverberating with shouts, laughter, chatter and tears.

I guess the flight, the ride from the airport and the noise had worn me down a bit because by the time I got to the reception desk, I was no longer thinking of the bright lights of Paris but rather of a café chair and a stiff drink. When the clerk handed me the key card and said "Room 1132," I snapped.

"No, absolutely not," I said. I wasn't even trying to speak in French. "Nothing higher than the fourth floor." The clerk looked at me quizzically. "I can't . . ." I said, then stopped. I didn't want to explain myself.

The authentic me? Well, here's a bit of authentic me. I'm claustrophobic; petrified of small, cramped spaces. And that makes elevators a challenge. Not too many people know this about me—I've made climbing the stairs seem like part of my dedication to a healthy lifestyle. Juan started referring to me as "the Stairmaster" after I'd climbed the stairs to an eighteenth-floor hospitality suite at an automotive convention. But the truth was I'd rather appear sweaty and winded in front of my colleagues than panic-stricken.

It took a few minutes for the clerk to find me a room on the fourth floor. Before I left the counter, she slid a small envelope across the surface with my room key. It must be from Antoine, I thought, dropping it in my pocket. I sent my bags up with the bellhop and headed for the stairs.

Once in the room, I kicked off my shoes and dropped onto the bed. I lay back and pulled the envelope from my pocket. It contained a single sheet of paper with this short note: "Antoine Gaucher, archivist," it said. "Catacombes de Paris, 1, avenue du Colonel Henri Rol-Tanguy. Meet me at my place of work, *s'il vous plaît*. Wednesday, 17:30 hours, after the museum closes."

Clearly, Antoine was not a chatty fellow.

Wednesday—that was tomorrow. I would have the whole day in Paris to myself. My first reaction was delight. A day to roam around one of the most spectacular cities on the planet. Where would I go? Notre Dame? Le Marais? Montmartre? The Louvre? But another thought began to nudge those places out of my mind. *A whole day.* I pulled my phone from my pocket. I had been away for two days, and I still had eight more talismans to collect. At this rate, how long would I be gone? Three weeks seemed possible, but very ambitious—and what if something went wrong? I tried to slow my breathing, loosen my clenched jaw. There was nothing I could do about the timing. Why worry about it, I told myself. Relax. Relax. Enjoy the opportunity you've been given. I took a deep breath and headed into the bathroom to clean up.

STROLLING DOWN THE Champs Élysées as the sun began to set, I felt wistful. Paris was really a place to be with someone else. I watched couples holding hands as they walked, men and women leaning close to each other as they sat at small tables in the outdoor cafés. If Annisha were here. . . If Annisha were here, we would have to talk about our relationship. What went wrong, how I was frustrating her, disappointing Adam. Damn. The magic of Paris was evaporating. Change tack. What would it be like to be here with Tessa? That was better. The romance of the unknown.

I walked a distance into the park, before turning around and heading back up the wide avenue. I could see the magnificent outline of the Arc de Triomphe in the distance. I stopped in one of the little bistros for dinner. I was ravenous. I ordered a salad and a carafe of red wine. Duck to follow, and then a selection of cheeses to end the meal. This was the way to eat.

The bistro was crowded. I tried to listen in on the conversations around me. A mother and daughter, clearly on vacation. What would they do tomorrow? Shopping or take the train to Versailles? Some businessmen talking about a presentation they would do at the end of the week. A couple talking about their neighbor's bad-tempered dog.

I lingered over the cheese tray for a long while, then paid my bill and headed back into the night. The sun had set, and the City of Lights was . . . alight. I made my way up the avenue to the Arc de Triomphe and climbed the three hundred or so stairs to the roof. I wouldn't be going up the Eiffel Tower (elevators), so this was the next best way to look at the city. Once at the top, I walked around the perimeter of the observation area.

The Eiffel Tower was shimmering to the west. Cars and cabs blinked their way down the streets radiating from the Place de l'Étoile. Tiny figures moved down the sidewalks, in and out of storefronts and doorways. So many people, so many lives; all different, all shifting and changing. Were all these souls living "authentic" lives? And if they weren't, would they know it?

I was still uncertain about what my authentic life was, but I had a suspicion I wasn't leading it. If I were, would there be so much that I wanted to avoid thinking about? Annisha? My father? Juan? If I were, wouldn't I be feeling a lot happier more of the time? I turned to head back down the stairs. Around and around the steps, the stone walls cool and silent. With each turn I felt energy draining from me. It had been a long day. A long several days, actually. Since meeting Julian, it had all been a whirlwind. My home, my work, seemed distant now. And the coming weeks loomed ahead like gigantic question marks. Time to head for the hotel bed; time for the forgetfulness of sleep.

THE NEXT MORNING, I took the metro to the Marais district of Paris, to a little café I remembered from a previous visit. A *café au lait* and a *pain au chocolat*. As I sat at the tiny table, I pulled out my phone. I answered a few messages and then switched to the Internet. I typed in "Catacombs of Paris."

I had heard about the catacombs but had never seen them. Reading about them now, that seemed like a very wise decision.

Like people in other Christian countries, Parisians buried their dead in the consecrated ground of the churchyards. The problem, apparently, was that as the centuries unfolded, these cemeteries began to fill. And of course, as time marched on, the populations who lived around the cemeteries grew. By the late 1700s the earth of the graveyards was choked with the victims of plague, epidemics, starvation and war. For decades, the corpses were piled one on top of the other, and the burial grounds spat bones and decomposing flesh through the mud. The air around these fields was rank; the oozing soil was contaminating the water and the food supplies. Diseased rats invaded homes and public space, and in one particularly grisly incident, the walls in a restaurant basement crumbled under the pressure of the rotting contents of the Saints Innocents Cemetery on the other side. Cadavers and bones flooded into the restaurant's cellar. I read that a mason inspecting the mess contracted gangrene after putting his hand on the remains of the cellar wall.

There must have been a public outcry during those years, but apparently it was that crumbling wall next to the Saints Innocents Cemetery that moved Parliament to close the cemetery and turned the mind of a police lieutenant, Alexandre Lenoir, toward a solution. Five years after the Innocents disaster, government officials acted on Lenoir's suggestion that the bodies from that cemetery and others throughout the city be transferred to the underground medieval stone quarries. The tunnels that lay south of the city gates were chosen, and the bones from Parisian cemeteries were exhumed and transported in elaborate processions to the newly consecrated ossuary. There was no way to preserve skeletons intact, so instead, bones were sorted by type and stacked and arranged along the tunnel walls together with grave markers taken from the original cemeteries. The catacombs, I learned, held the remains of six million people.

As I read, I looked at a few pictures and was relieved that

Antoine had asked me to meet him after the catacombs had
been closed for the day. There was no way that I would be taking a tour. Bad enough to spend time with piles of bones, but
small, dark tunnels. . . I felt a little lightheaded just thinking
about that.

After breakfast, I wandered through the streets. By mid-
morning the sun was hot, beating down through a clear spring
sky. The brilliance and the pulsing warmth reminded me of
the "authenticity" talisman—that little sun and moon coin.
It was supposed to have some sort of restorative power. How
exactly did that work? Did it help you become your truest self?
And if it did, how was that healing? As I walked, I looked at
the faces around me. I started playing a little game, identi-
fying each person I passed as living their authentic life—or
not. The tall young man with his nose buried deep in a Paris
guidebook—not. The child clutching a small stuffed dog—
authentic. The middle-aged waiter who stood in the doorway
of a small bistro, pulling on a cigarette and scowling—not.
The woman putting up a display of brightly colored scarves
in a shop window—authentic. I kept at this for several blocks
before I started to wonder what was making me come to those
conclusions. It was, I thought, a certain look of contentment
on the faces of the people which made me feel they were living their "real" lives versus constructing some plastic life that
society had convinced them to inhabit. A look that suggested
they were sure of who they were, what was important to them
and what their days stood for. Who else had that look? I think
my mom and dad had it. Maybe that's just a child's assump-
tion, but even when they would grumble about our cramped
house or our clunker of a car, they seemed undisturbed, always

utterly satisfied, in fact. It drove me crazy. I thought of a few friends, and then Juan's face popped into my mind. Not Juan of the most recent years, but the Juan I had met when I first walked through the doors of the company.

JUAN MUST HAVE BEEN in his early forties when I met him, but he had the wise expression and intellectual enthusiasm of an old scholar. During my interview with Juan, he had seemed distracted, indifferent even; so I was surprised when he called to offer me the job. I would come to recognize that, during the interview, I had simply witnessed Juan lost in thought. Apparently he was so impressed with my aptitude tests, my previous work experience and my opening remarks that he was thinking ahead to what projects he could assign to me. On my first day, however, I was greeted with a thoroughly engaged Juan.

"There he is!" he announced as I hovered in the doorway. "Come, everyone," he said to those scattered around the lab. "Come meet the new member of our team—the young but impressive Jonathan Landry."

There were introductions and a tour, a team lunch afterward at a local greasy spoon. Juan had me start in right away, working on a redesign. I spent the afternoon hunched over a computer screen, conscious with every second that ticked by of how much I wanted to succeed. At about five o'clock I felt a hand on my shoulder. I looked up to see Juan smiling at me. "I'd say that was a pretty busy first day, wouldn't you?" he said. "I've got some paperwork to finish up, but you should head home. Good work." It hardly felt as if I had accomplished anything, but Juan's confidence in me was reassuring.

I took a deep breath, saved my work and then shut down the computer.

The entire week proceeded like that. I would be sitting over the computer, concentrating intensely, and just as my shoulders started to cramp or a headache began to dig into my temples, Juan would appear at my side to ask how I was doing or to offer a suggestion, or even, on occasion, to suggest I take a short break. But despite all his support, I managed to blunder before my very first month was out—a careless miscalculation that had sample plans rejected. Juan's boss had marched into the lab and flung a sheaf of papers onto one of the counters. "Whose work is this?" he demanded. Juan appeared immediately, picked up the papers and scanned them.

"Many apologies, Karl," he replied. "I can see we made an error here. I'll be sure to get you corrected plans by the end of the day." Karl hovered a moment, casting a suspicious glance in my direction. "My mistake," said Juan, moving toward the door, clearly trying to get Karl out of the lab. "But it's a quick fix. We'll get at it immediately."

After Karl disappeared down the hallway, Juan came over to my workstation. "Just shows that we can't be too careful in our work," he said as he dropped the report down in front of me. "But you should never be afraid of making mistakes," he added. "It's how we learn."

That was Juan in a nutshell. No blaming me or the fellow who had checked my work before it went out. Calm and philosophical. Unfailingly positive. Supportive of everyone who worked for him. He got the best out of us. I truly believe that.

Back then I couldn't have guessed that, eight years later, Juan would be gone. And before Juan disappeared completely, a harried, harassed version of the man would be all that was left. His shoulders stooped, his face pinched, his hair an astonishing shock of gray. I would no longer be working for him, but worse still, I would no longer be speaking to him.

THE APPEARANCE OF THE SEINE interrupted my thoughts of Juan. I had arrived at the Notre Dame bridge. I headed across and then wandered the streets until I reached the cathedral. I stood for a long time outside those magnificent doors, the stone walls peopled with saints and gargoyles, the glass of the rose window flashing in the sun. What breathtaking work. What a humbling accomplishment. I took out my phone and snapped a couple of photos to show Adam when I got home. Then I headed in.

I spent the rest of the day walking and hopping on and off the metro, hitting the tourist spots, exploring the streets of the Latin Quarter, eventually stopping for a late afternoon rest in a bistro called Les Deux Magots near Boulevard Saint-Germain. The sky had become overcast, but I still chose a table outside. I ordered a *citron pressé* and leaned back on my cane chair. I put my hand over the little pouch that hung under my shirt and watched the pedestrians file past. It had been a pleasant day, but now I felt my heart sag in my chest. I was on my own—and for how long, I had no idea. I wanted to be back home. Adam would come for the weekend. I would be with people all week at the office. Maybe I would get up my nerve to ask Tessa to lunch. Or dinner. That would be a good way to avoid my empty apartment for a while. The thought of her dark curls made me smile.

I could have sat there until the sun set, but my phone beeped at me, reminding me that I had to be at the catacombs soon. I paid the bill and reluctantly headed out to the metro.

After a short ride, I exited at the Denfert-Rochereau metro stop and climbed the stairs. I stumbled around the parkette at Place Denfert-Rochereau, looking for signs, and soon made my way to a stone building that I had read was part of the former Barrière d'Enfer city gate. The short dark structure attached to it appeared to be the ticket office of the catacombs. But the small door was firmly shut, and there was no one around. I knocked and waited, but no answer. I knocked again, this time drumming hard on the dark wood. I thought I heard footsteps on the other side, and then the door slowly opened inward. A pimply young man of about eighteen was standing in front of me.

"Antoine?" I asked doubtfully.

"*Non*," said the fellow, rolling his eyes. "*Il travaille. Suivez-moi.*" He turned and walked into the building, and I had no choice but to follow. He was walking quickly, so I had to hurry behind him.

"*Où est . . .*" I began in my limited French. My guide waved his hand dismissively and repeated, "*Suivez-moi.*" After a few steps, he disappeared through a stone doorway. When I reached the threshold, I saw with horror that it opened onto a set of steep stone stairs—spiraling down. The catacombs. We were heading into the tunnels. My heart leaped in my chest, my shirt collar felt tight, air seemed to be blocked from my lungs. But despite the rising panic, my feet were pounding down the narrow stone stairs, the sound only slightly louder than my thumping heart. Down, down, down we went. My head was spinning, the constant turning around the stairs was making me feel nauseated. I had no idea how far down we were going, but by the time the stairs ended, it felt as if we were several stories underground.

My wordless guide was moving quickly ahead of me, as if he too disliked being down here. The tunnel was damp, and dimly lit. The bones of six million Parisians were entombed in this place. But I hadn't seen any skeletons yet, and it wasn't the dead that were haunting me. It was the tunnel, the low ceilings, the tight walls. As I hurried behind my escort, I felt my breath become increasingly shallow and rapid. Beads of perspiration were forming on my brow, although I was shivering. Waves of dizziness were washing over me, and it was an effort to put one foot ahead of the other. I didn't know if I could go on, but the thought of losing sight of the young man kept me going. I knew I needed to distract myself.

Just then, we passed a small recess that was walled off with Plexiglas. Behind the barrier were a worn wooden chair and a small table with a candle on it. A plaque on the wall said something about the Second World War. I remembered another thing I had read about the catacombs. During the war, resistance fighters had hidden in these winding networks of tunnels. Spent years down here, in fact.

What would it have been like to have worked against the Nazi stranglehold? Did French resistance fighters live in a constant state of fear and foreboding? Or did their commitment to their cause, to justice, to freedom, imbue them with courage? It was probably both sets of feelings, I realized. True bravery can happen only in the face of fear—if you aren't afraid, then how can your actions be brave?

But what irony. Living in these small, cramped spaces, surrounded by relics of the dead, testaments to inevitable mortality, did the fighters ever look upon the bones and think that, whatever the resistance did, everyone they were trying to save would end up here? Did it matter if they slowed human suffering and needless death? Did it make any of them doubt their struggle, wonder if it was all worth it? The bones in these tunnels belonged to people whose lives had passed by—some with great meaning and significance, others without. Did it matter, really, which way they had lived? Which way anyone lived?

My guide was continuing to snake ahead of me. I picked up my pace just in time to turn the corner and face the first stack of bones.

Despite myself, I slowed my pace. My panic had ebbed. The long, sloping walls were encased with bones—neat stacks of femurs, precise piles of tibias. Intricate, ornate patterns were spelled out in clavicles and ribs. Directly ahead of me was a column of grinning skulls. I thought of those hiding in the catacombs. Of course it mattered how people lived. The resistance fighters knew that. They must have looked at these bones and realized that the horrors underground were nothing compared to the horrors that were being committed above them, in the occupied streets of Paris, of Lodz, of Berlin, of Amsterdam. All resistance fighters, wherever they lived, must have realized that it would be better to face the terror than try to ignore it.

Suddenly the young man stopped at the entranceway of a new tunnel. It was separated from the one we had followed by a piece of rusted iron fencing. The tunnel was dark. My guide moved the fence to one side and turned into the blackness. He paused and looked behind at me, making sure I was following.

I moved uncertainly out of the anemic light as his back disappeared in front of me. I took a few more steps. Then my foot knocked against something. A wooden rattle filled the air, and I froze. As I did, light flared around me. My guide had snapped on his flashlight. Suddenly I wished he hadn't. The gruesome orderliness was gone. Bones were everywhere—scattered across the floor around our feet, cascading from loose stacks against the walls. The glare from the flashlight caught on waves of dust and tendrils of cobwebs that hung from the ceiling.

"*Ça c'est pour vous,*" said my guide. He thrust the flashlight at me. As I took it, he brushed past me.

"What—" I began to call out.

Before I could finish my question, the man snapped, "*Il vous rencontrera ici.*" And then he was gone, leaving me alone, fifty feet underground, a solitary human being standing in a sea of the dead.

There was nothing to distract me now. The air was still but the tunnel walls seemed to be squeezing in on me. The ceiling appeared to shudder—I was sure that, at any moment, it would come crashing down. *This isn't real,* I tried to tell myself. *This is an anxiety attack.* But panic was beating through me, threatening to tear me apart. I wanted to lean against something, to hold myself up, but I was too afraid to move through the bones.

After what seemed like hours but was probably only a few seconds, I heard the sound of footsteps.

A small man appeared out of the shadows. "*C'est moi, Antoine,*" the figure announced. Just as he did, I began to sway.

"*Mon dieu!*" said Antoine. He grabbed my arm and steadied me. Then he moved to a gap between the piles of bones along the wall. He retrieved two small folding stools and brought them to the middle of the tunnel, unfolding them on the uneven ground.

"*Asseyez-vous,*" he said. "Sit, sit."

Antoine was probably in his fifties, white curly hair surrounding a pale, wrinkled face. He wore small round glasses and something that approached a dark lab coat. Like Ahmet, he had a kind face, but there was a studious air about him.

"I apologize for making you wait here for me," said Antoine. "I'm working this evening—restoration. Gradually, the bones settle, fall over. And there have been incidents of vandalism. It is a constant effort."

My breathing was beginning to slow. The one good thing about my panic attacks was that they didn't last long. It was as if my body simply couldn't sustain the energy they required. I wiped my brow and muttered, "It's okay."

Antoine nodded and smiled gently. "I'm not surprised you don't like it down here," he said. "Most people are okay until the place empties. They don't really want to be alone with their thoughts down here, the way I am each day. But you know, we grow fearless by doing those things we fear." He patted his pockets and pulled out a small tin. Lifting the lid, he offered me a candy. I shook my head, and he popped one in his mouth before settling the tin back in his pocket. "As a very young boy, I lost my father," he said. "Everything I knew about him was from the past—perhaps that's why I became so interested in history, in archives. But the sight of him in his coffin haunted me for years. Haunted me. When this job opened up, I thought, *No, no working with bones, with the dead. That's the last thing I want to do.* But then I realized that it was precisely because

I feared the dead that I should take this job. It has been," he laughed, waving his hands around, "liberating."

Then he leaned forward and stared at me. "Are you feeling better?" he asked. I nodded.

"Oh," he said then, as if remembering something. "Here." He handed me a small parcel and a square of folded parchment, like the one Ahmet had given me in Turkey. "I have to continue working," he said. "But I know you won't mind leaving me now, will you?" I shook my head and attempted a smile, a little surprised at the brevity of the meeting I'd traveled so far for. We both stood up. "I think you can find your way out," Antoine said. He moved toward the metal barrier and pointed down the dimly lit tunnel. "That way," he said. "Just follow the tunnel and don't go down any of the offshoots that are fenced off. I've asked Jean to leave the door open so you can let yourself out."

I had pocketed the package and the parchment. "Thank you," I said, as I moved past Antoine. "Thank you."

As I hurried down the tunnel, I heard Antoine call out, "Courage, Jonathan! That's the only way to live. And remember, bravery isn't really something you feel. It's something you show."

I moved through the tunnels. The symmetry, the neatness, the intricate arrangement of bones was a relief compared to the raw mess of Antoine's tunnel. If I hadn't been so anxious to get out of the tight space, I would have lingered to admire the artistry. Instead, I took deep breaths and reminded myself that the end was just around the corner, or the next one. Eventually, I made my way to the bottom of another stone staircase. I climbed up as quickly as I could, my legs aching slightly from yesterday's Arc de Triomphe climb. When I reached the top,

I moved outside with relief. The fresh evening air was like a blessing. I took several greedy gulps before I headed down the sidewalk toward a bench.

I lowered myself onto the seat and turned my attention to the small bundle that Antoine had handed me. I peeled back several layers of yellowed tissue paper. At the center of the tissue was a tiny metal skull. The jaws of the skull were parted, making it appear to be grinning at me. Or laughing. That made me smile. I turned the miniature skull over in my hands. Antiqued bronze, perhaps. Or some sort of iron alloy. I took the leather pouch from around my neck and dropped the talisman in. Then I carefully unfolded the parchment.

*Embrace Your Fears* was the title. I chuckled. Of course this talisman would be about fear. I continued to read:

*What holds us back in life is the invisible architecture of fear. It keeps us in our comfort zones, which are, in truth, the least safe places in which to live. Indeed, the greatest risk in life is taking no risks. But every time we do that which we fear, we take back the power that fear has stolen from us—for on the other side of our fears lives our strength. Every time we step into the discomfort of growth and progress, we become more free. The more fears we walk through, the more power we reclaim. In this way, we grow both fearless and powerful, and thus are able to live the lives of our dreams.*

I pulled the notebook from my jacket pocket and tucked the parchment inside. Then I put the pouch back around my neck and headed for the metro.

It was not quite six-thirty. My whole catacomb ordeal had

taken less than an hour. In the afternoon I had received a message from Julian, saying there would be a plane ticket waiting for me at the terminal the next morning. I had the whole evening before me. I decided that I would return to the hotel and clean up a bit. Then I would head for Place du Trocadéro, across the river from the Eiffel Tower. I would have dinner in a restaurant there, and then watch the lights of the tower before I headed for bed.

I got off the metro at the Charles de Gaulle Étoile station and headed down the Champs Élysées. I was lost in thought the whole way back, thinking about my dark moments in the tunnel, my panic and my survival. When I got to the hotel lobby, I headed over to the elevator. When the doors opened, I stepped in and pressed "four." I looked out through the doors, toward the lobby, but I didn't move. The doors slowly slid shut. And then the elevator started to lift. This was the first time I had taken an elevator in twenty years. I was terrified. But it felt okay.

# Chapter Five

I HAD TRIED TO REACH JULIAN several times while in Paris, but his phone remained unanswered. No explanation of where I might be heading, or of whom I was to meet, or about how long I would be. I clenched my teeth. I deserved some details, some information. I called him one more time, but there was no answer.

So there I was the following morning, standing like an idiot in front of the startled Air France check-in attendant, my eyes bulging and my voice suddenly hitting the heights of a soprano. "Osaka?" I squeaked. "Japan? Are you kidding me?"

I don't know why this particular destination should have rattled me. I suppose it was the prospect of putting my already jet-lagged body on a twelve-hour flight. My head hurt just thinking about going off to yet another place I had never before been, about dropping into a country where I knew no one and spoke not one word of the language.

As I shuffled down the aisle on the plane, I realized with despair that I was in a middle seat—a middle seat in the middle aisle. On one side of me was a large man who immediately commandeered the armrest. On the other, a slight woman who quickly pulled a book out of her bag and rested it on the pull-out seat table: the international sign for "don't talk to me." That was fine by me. I was in no mood to chat.

I thought I too might read or watch a movie, but my mind was racing about, touching on everything that had happened over the past few days. And I couldn't seem to get comfortable. It wasn't just the fellow spilling over the seat next to me or the jet of cool air blasting past my right ear, courtesy of my other neighbor's efforts to adjust the overhead fan. My clothes felt tight and itchy, my throat dry, and the leather pouch that held the talismans seemed to be digging its cord into my neck again. With some difficulty, I got the thing out from under my shirt. I put it into my pants pocket, but I couldn't seem to position it in a way that would keep it from jutting into my hip. My carry-on was now buried in the overhead compartment, and I didn't want to put the pouch in the seat pocket in front of me. I was sure I would accidentally leave it there when I got off the plane. As I was fiddling with my pockets, shifting around in my seat, the woman next to me sighed audibly. That annoyed me, but she was right. I was making a nuisance of myself. I put the cord around my neck and stuffed the pouch back under my shirt.

Six hours into the flight, I began to brood about what lay ahead. I would be arriving in Osaka in the early morning, although it would be late at night on the Paris clock. I would miss an entire night of sleep. What's more, I had six hours stretching ahead of me, six more hours in this cramped space. The only solution, I thought, would be to take a nap—hoping a few hours of sleep would both hurry the trip and make my first day in Japan bearable. Clearly other people around me had the same idea. The fellow next to me had nodded off; the woman on the other side had finished her book and was reclining her seat and closing her eyes. In fact, everyone around me seemed to have fallen silent. Everyone, that is, except two young women directly behind me.

They were speaking in English. During the course of the first few hours of the flight, I had overheard one of them saying she was heading to Osaka to teach English as a second language. The other young woman had explained, in French-accented English, that she had relatives living in Osaka. She was going to use their place as base for a three-month trek through Asia. They had been exchanging bits and pieces of information, but at the halfway mark of the trip they seemed to hit a new level of intimacy. The conversation was now imbued with an energy and enthusiasm—and a *volume*—that might have been more appropriate in a noisy nightclub than in a crowded plane. I tried to ignore their talk, but I couldn't. I pulled out my airline headphones and put them on. I flipped stations, looking for one that was playing soothing music, but nothing could quite drown out the percussion of voices behind me. I couldn't figure out how the guy next to me was snoring through the racket.

The hours stretched on and on. I heard about cheating partners and fair-weather friends. About awesome yoga classes and tasteful tattoos. About hair extensions and deep colon cleansing. By the time they hit their plans for the future, I was feeling homicidal. Eventually I reconciled myself to a string of comedies on the movie channel, but the second-rate hijinks did nothing to lighten my mood.

When I finally stumbled off the plane half a day after I had first shuffled on, an impossibly tedious twelve hours of recycled air and leg cramps behind me, I was in a fog, beyond rational thought. Not knowing what else to do, I followed the crowd until I ended up wedged in a mass of bodies pressing toward the baggage carousels.

I was fully aware that there was no real need to squeeze in around the conveyor belt yet. Sometimes airline baggage arrives so slowly, it seems it came over on the *Queen Mary* rather than on the same plane you had been flying on.

I moved over to a wall and slid down until I was squatting. Then I pulled my phone from my pocket and turned it on.

I noticed immediately a message from Julian.

*Dear Jonathan,*

*So sorry not to have been available when you called, and not to have given you more details. I did leave a message with the name of the next safekeeper and instructions, but it sounds as if that call somehow went missing from your hotel system. At any rate, you will be staying with a delightful young woman named Sato Ayame (Ayame is her first name) at her family's inn in Kyoto. She will meet you at the airport. Enjoy your time in Japan.*

*Have fun,*
*Julian*

I sent Annisha and Adam a message, telling them I had landed in Osaka, and then placed the phone back in my pocket. As I did, a familiar voice caught my ears.

"It's just been so great getting to know you!" The voice was coming from one of two young women standing shoulder to shoulder in front of the baggage carousel. My incessantly chatty neighbors. I felt a headache ratcheting up. There seemed to be nothing happening with the baggage, so I stood up and escaped down the hall to find a bathroom. By the time I had returned, bags were clunking down from the chute and making their way around the conveyor belt. The dark-haired girl was leaning over the baggage, pulling a pink plaid duffel bag off the belt. I moved closer to the carousel. After watching one revolution, I could see that my bag had not yet fallen, so I turned my eye to the chute. Twenty minutes later I was still there, still willing my luggage to come cascading down toward me. But it was clear there was nothing left to disgorge. I turned my attention back to the few bags that remained on the revolving circuit. But as much as I wished it, my own was not among them.

I had a toothbrush and one pair of clean underwear in my carry-on, but all my toiletries and most of my belongings were in that absent baggage. I could feel tension squeezing my temples. My head was thumping, my chest tight. *Why me?* I thought. A million miles away from home, without my stuff. And now facing an enormous hassle.

Most of the crowd from my flight had disappeared. I looked around the area. The Kansai airport was new, bright and sleek, but like so many large airports it had a labyrinthine feel—a confusing vastness that made it seem both crowded and chillingly empty. The signs were in Japanese and English, but the

English looked abbreviated. I was beginning to despair of figuring out where I should go or what I should do. And there was still customs and immigration to navigate before I could exit the area and find Ayame.

The long flight, the nattering passengers, my deep fatigue— it was as if a little switch had been thrown. In an instant, I was no longer anxious, but in a rage. My heart was pounding and my limbs felt twitchy, as if electricity were running through my veins. I noticed a man standing some distance off, in a uniform that looked like it might have been airport issue. I almost lunged at him.

In retrospect, I see how enormously lucky I was. It is not a wise idea to lose your temper in an airport these days. It was a miracle I wasn't hauled off to some interrogation room or, worse yet, arrested. But somehow or other, I was escorted through customs and immigration, was introduced to the airline employee who promised to find my luggage, and was courteously deposited in the arrivals meeting area, shaking and spent. Before all that, however, I had unloaded my mind, in English and a few halting bits of French, to everyone who would listen. I had to wonder if a language barrier kept most of what I said a bit of a mystery to the people who had helped me. It seemed hard to imagine that simple politeness or kindness could keep anyone from telling me what I could do with myself and my missing baggage.

My temper tantrum, and all the ensuing maneuvers, had left me feeling hollow and frail. All I wanted to do was collapse in a car and be chauffeured to a comfortable bed. I looked around the arrivals area desperately. Standing several yards away, near some seats and a bank of phones, was a woman of about thirty. She had shiny neck-length hair and wore a bright green shirt and faded jeans. She wasn't holding a sign as Ahmet had been, but she was clearly looking for someone. When our eyes met, she cocked her head and walked toward me. As she got close, she smiled. "*Hajime-mashite. Jonathan Landry-sama?*" she asked. I nodded, and she bent at the waist to give me a little bow.

I thought back to when I had moved into sales, and the firm had sent me to a seminar on business etiquette in other countries. I had forgotten nearly everything, but now I realized that, in my hour in the Kansai airport, I had probably broken every rule of Japanese civility. It really was a marvel that I had been treated with such patience. Now I bowed in return, trying to make it a little deeper than Ayame's.

"Welcome to Japan," Ayame said. "It is a great honor to meet you."

"Oh thank God! You speak English," I said before I could stop myself.

Ayame bowed again and smiled.

"Yes," she said. "I teach English literature at Kyoto University, so it's something of a prerequisite."

I tried to recover myself by apologizing for my comment about her English and explaining my relief. "It's just that they've lost my luggage," I told Ayame. "I need to go back to the airline desk and give them an address where they can send it when they find it."

Ayame accompanied me to the airline counter. She asked for my permission to do the talking—an offer I gratefully accepted. My nerves were still raw. I didn't trust myself not to fly off the handle again.

Ayame talked to the attendant in Japanese. When she turned from the counter she told me that my baggage had been located and was on a later flight to Osaka. It would be sent by courier to the inn in Kyoto as soon as it arrived. She then started walking down the long glass-walled corridor. I expected to be led to the car park, but Ayame said we would be taking the train from the airport station to Kyoto, and then a cab to her parents' *ryokan* in East Kyoto.

"A *ryokan*," she explained, "is a traditional Japanese inn. I hope you will find it comfortable. Many travelers enjoy the change from Western-style hotels."

THE TRAIN WAS CROWDED, but Ayame and I found two seats together. As we settled ourselves, she told me that the ride would take about an hour and a half. I couldn't stifle a deep sigh. Ayame looked at me with a raised eyebrow.

"I'm sorry. I'm not deliberately trying to be offensive. It's just that I'm so tired from all this travel. I don't even know what time it is—or what day of the week! And this still seems ridiculous to me. I just don't understand why you 'safekeepers,' or whatever Julian likes to call you, can't mail these things back."

"I know that Julian must have good reasons for wanting to do things this way," Ayame replied. "Perhaps what you need to do is just be a little more philosophic about the adventure. After all," she added gently, "life is a journey. . . ."

"Yeah, yeah," I couldn't stop myself now, "but this isn't a journey. This is some kind of messed-up fun-house ride. I've been all over the flipping world in the last little while . . . Buenos Aires,

Istanbul, Paris ... and God knows where I'll be tomorrow or next week."

"Umm, yes. That's difficult," Ayame said gently. "But you know what they say? It doesn't matter where you are going, just who you are becoming."

But I was in no mood for homilies.

"What is it with you people?" I snapped. "You all sound the same. You all sound like Julian."

Ayame looked bemused rather than annoyed.

"Does that surprise you? We are all good friends of Julian. We have all learned so much from him. We have all changed our lives because of him," she said.

"Well, my life is changing, too," I said, "but I'm not so sure it's going to be for the better. Everything's going to hell at work. And my wife. . ."

I stopped there. I didn't want to talk about that. I didn't want to think about all the things that were missing from life. My wife. My son. My luggage.

After a moment of quiet, Ayame spoke up again.

"You must be worried too about Julian," she said.

"What?" I said.

"That he has asked you to collect the talismans. That he needs them. Are you worried about why he needs them? About the person he needs to help?"

I hadn't been thinking much about that lately. What if Julian wasn't telling the truth about my mother? What if my mother was ill? My mother is one of those people who generally makes life look effortless. I think I was about twelve before I realized that she got sick like everyone else.

If it wasn't Mom, maybe it was my sister, Kira. Although

she was two years younger than me, I always thought of her as the responsible one. She was the one who watched over Mom when Dad died, who reminded me of Mom's birthday or told me when Mom needed a phone call or a visit. She was the one who kept in touch with me, who did all the heavy lifting in the relationship. Would she even tell me if she was sick or in trouble? And then there were my aunts, uncles and cousins.

And even if the person who needed Julian's help wasn't a family member, did that mean I shouldn't be thinking about the importance of this task I'd been sent out to do? I had been utterly self-absorbed for the past few days.

"Yes," I said, although it wasn't really honest, "that has been weighing on my mind, too."

Several minutes passed before Ayame said anything.

"It's almost eight in the morning, by the way," she said. Then she added, "Perhaps you would like this opportunity to rest."

The train, in pleasant contrast to the plane, was quiet. There was only the muted hum of voices somewhere in the far distance. I closed my eyes and relaxed into the gentle vibration. Before I knew it, I was asleep.

I DON'T THINK I LOOKED once at Ayame as we traveled down the Kyoto streets in a taxi. Arriving at the Kyoto train station had been like stepping into sleek, urban Japan—what I imagine Tokyo to be like. High-vaulted ceilings, sweeping arches of glass and metal, everything gleaming and pristine, bright and spare. And the Kyoto cityscape looked like almost any other modern city—against rolling hills on the horizon, glass-paneled skyscrapers mixed with nondescript buildings and towers of various sizes. There was even one of those disk-topped towers—like the Space Needle in Seattle. But now that we were threading through the streets themselves, everything looked different. Squeezed between modern brick buildings were small wooden houses, some with curled tiled roofs, many with wooden peaks and ornate trim. A number had lush planters out front with vines and bonsai trees. I noticed several women walking down the street in kimonos.

"There is much history, much to see in Kyoto," said Ayame. "It was once the capital of all Japan. And it escaped the bombing and destruction of the Second World War. Many, many temples here."

"Is that so?" I said, still staring out the window.

"Maybe tomorrow, I can take you to see one."

"Yes, that would be great, if there's time."

"And tonight," said Ayame, "my parents would like you to join us for dinner. A traditional *kaiseki* meal."

I hesitated before I replied.

"I would enjoy that," I said, "but I have to warn you in advance. I know that you do things differently from where I come from, that the etiquette is complicated." I was having trouble saying what I meant. I was thinking about the airport scene. "I'm afraid that I may insult people."

"Please don't worry," Ayame replied. "I understand that, my parents understand that. But I'll explain things as we go along, if you'd like."

I nodded. Just then, the taxi pulled over to the side of the road.

"We have to get out here," said Ayame. "The inn is down that street." She pointed just ahead of us to what looked like an alley. "It is a very old street. Too narrow for cars."

We stepped out of the cab and turned down the lane. The stones that paved it were a little slick, and the air was warm and damp—as if it had just rained. The street was filled with modest shops and cramped doorways in an unbroken line. We walked for only a short distance before we got to what looked like a small wooden house sandwiched between the other buildings. Its curved roof was lined with dark brown cylindrical tiles, its windows latticed in dark wood. Low stone walls curved on either side of a carved wooden double door; leafy branches spilled over their tops.

"This is one of the oldest *ryokan* in the city," said Ayame. "It's been run by members of my family for many generations. But it is small. Just eleven rooms and my parents' apartment."

She pulled at one of the doors and ushered me in.

We entered a modest slate-tiled hallway. Several pairs of shoes were lined up along the wall. Just beyond, a low step led into a lobby area. An assortment of cream-colored slippers were lined up at one side of the step.

"Please," said Ayame. "Place your shoes here and find a pair of slippers your size."

We both took off our shoes, put on slippers and then stepped into the lobby. As we did, a man and a woman came around the corner. "My parents," announced Ayame.

There was much bowing and smiling during the introductions, with Ayame translating as we attempted to say hello to one another. Eventually Ayame's father turned to her and said something to her in a grave tone of voice.

"Oh yes," said Ayame. "My father is reminding me that you've had a very long journey and a difficult morning and that you must need to rest. I will take you to your room."

As I STRETCHED OUT on the low futon, I couldn't believe how much more relaxed I felt than I had just an hour before. Ayame had shown me my room and then led me to a men's *ofuro*, or bath, down the hall.

"There will be a robe for you inside, and towels and toiletries on a small shelf beside the door," she said. "Shower first, and then soak in the tub for as long as you like. I will place a note on the door to say that the room is occupied."

The room I entered was small—a floor of tiny white tiles, wooden walls lined with three hand-held shower faucets. In front of each shower stood a small wooden stool and a bucket. In the corner farthest away from the door was a square wooden hot tub. The walls of the tub rose about a foot above the floor, but it was clear that the bottom of the bath was sunken far below ground level. The room was warm and humid and filled with a lovely lemony scent I later discovered was *hinoki*, Japanese cypress. The oil in the wood is said to be very therapeutic.

A few minutes later I lowered myself into the bath. The water reached almost to my chin. I leaned back against the wooden side and breathed deeply. Fragrant steam rose from the hot water. The heat stung my skin slightly, but I could feel it melting away the knots in my shoulders and back.


THERE WAS NO DOUBT about it—this was a strange trip. It was confusing and tiring, but it was also making me struggle in less obvious ways. These notes that accompanied the talismans—I knew they were not written for me specifically, that Julian had composed them for his own purposes. But he had suggested I read them and had given me a journal for my thoughts. He must have anticipated how the notes would affect me.

That first talisman: <u>authenticity</u>. Being true to yourself. That idea had really got under my skin, and I was beginning to suspect why. There was something about my life that wasn't quite right. It was more than the fact that I had disappointed Annisha and Adam. To fix this problem would take more than saying sorry to Annisha, making it home for dinner more often, attending a few more soccer practices with Adam. I was beginning to realize that my shortcomings as a parent or as a husband were being buttressed by a deep unhappiness. But it wasn't an unhappiness with Annisha or Adam. It was an unhappiness with the texture of my life. It was as if I had taken all my ambition and drive and focused it on a race I had no real interest in winning. I was moving ahead, but I wasn't going where I wanted to go. I love engineering. I love circuitry. I love mathematical challenges. I love technical design. And I'm good at these things. When I was in the design lab, I felt my work had purpose and my life made sense. There was nothing wrong with sales, but I just didn't feel the same passion in that world.

Now, lying here in the tranquil *ryokan* room, I knew I was getting closer to what my authentic life might be. I could see that I had to make some serious changes. It was a scary thought, but I felt surprisingly peaceful about it. As if it were all in the distant future.

AYAME HAD LEFT a small pile of clothes on the end of the futon while I had been having my bath. There was a note: "I borrowed these from a friend. I hope they fit."

I got up off the bed and took off my robe. Then I pulled on the soft cotton golf shirt, a pair of loose-fitting khakis. There was also a pair of white sport socks still in their package. I put those on as well, before placing my feet back in the slippers. Then I picked up my journal and a pen from the nightstand and shuffled over to the far side of the room.

The guest room was small but airy. Tatami mats covered the floor. The white walls were set off with a dark wood framework that made them look a little like the paper screens that lined the lobby area. Near the foot of the bed was a small low table. On two sides of it were legless chairs—seat and back cushions that sat directly on the floor. Beyond were mullioned floor-to-ceiling windows, with a sliding door that led out onto a green area. I opened the door and stepped out onto a little wooden veranda. Although I could see the greenery of a garden through the window while resting on the futon, I wasn't prepared for what greeted me outside.

The veranda ran around three sides of a deep and lush garden. Clearly all the rooms were centered around this quiet courtyard. In the middle of the garden was a tall stone statue of a many-storied pagoda. Smaller statues were sprinkled throughout the greenery—several cranes, a Buddha, a rather threatening-looking toad. And at the far end of the garden, I could see a tiny waterfall cascading over a stone ledge. The burbling sound suggested that a pool was beneath it, hidden from my view by leaves and branches. The leaves and branches, in fact, hid all parts of the ground from view. The base of each delicate tree was surrounded by bright green ferns; arching branches with tiny flowers graced the carefully sculpted bushes.

There was a wooden folding chair next to where I stood. I

moved over and sat down. I dropped the journal onto my lap and stared into the green space as the minutes slipped by.

The toad sculpture appeared to have a sinister smile and reminded me of the little grinning skull I had received from Antoine. *Embrace your fears,* the accompanying note had said. Well, I had already done a number of things I feared—including leaving my family and my job behind for this scavenger hunt. I had jumped off the edge of a cliff in a way. But I had been whining and complaining about it the whole time. I suppose by "embrace your fear," Julian meant that a person should embrace it in a positive fashion, move out of one's safe harbor; that a person should be exhilarated by the unknown, not become hysterical. Not long ago, I had taken a ride in an elevator for the first time in twenty years. But what else should I be doing?

Well, my biggest fears—losing my family, losing Annisha, losing Adam—were not things I wanted to embrace. And I don't think that was what Julian's note meant. But I couldn't help seeing the irony. The things I feared most were happening in my life despite all my caution. And they were being realized precisely because I had been passive. Maybe if I had made some of the changes Annisha suggested—turned down a promotion or two, or switched positions, or just said no once in a while, things I was too frightened to do—I wouldn't be facing this crisis. And what if I went really deep? What did I really want to do that I was afraid of? I was beginning to see that doing things you are frightened of may just make life less scary in the long run.

Just as I was finished writing these thoughts in the journal, I heard a gentle knock coming from my room. It was Ayame, coming to tell me that she had my luggage.

"By the way," she added, "have you checked your phone? I

just noticed that Julian copied me on a note he sent to you with your itinerary for the next few days. Your most unusual trip will definitely continue. Lucky you."

DINNER TURNED OUT TO BE a long, elaborate event. I was ushered into the Satos' private reception room, where Ayame's parents were waiting. After we greeted one another with smiles and bows, they gestured toward the table. It was low, like the one in my room, and on each of the four sides was a large white cotton cushion. I noticed a little alcove at the side of the room, backed with a beautiful scroll-like ink drawing of cranes and water reeds. Small sculptures and a simple flower arrangement were positioned in front of the drawing. I started to head toward the pillow opposite the alcove—I thought it would provide a pleasant view—but Ayame shook her head gently and led me to the side of the table that faced the other way.

"It is considered immodest to seat guests across from one's *tokonoma*. It would be like bragging—like saying, 'Look what lovely things we have.'"

"I see," I said. I must have sounded disappointed because Ayame added, "I would let you sit there, but it would make my parents very uncomfortable. I hope you understand."

After we were seated, a young woman came in with a tray of hot, damp towels.

"*Oshibori*," Ayame said. "For cleaning your hands. But do not use it like a Western napkin. You shouldn't wipe your mouth or your face with it."

When the first course was brought out and served, Ayame and her parents said, in unison, "*Itadakimasu*."

"It means 'I humbly receive,'" Ayame explained. "We start that way and end the meal with *gochisosama-deshita,* which means 'thank you for a good meal.'"

Dinner lasted long into the evening. There was soup and sushi and sashimi; tempura and steamed fish; and broiled beef and pickled vegetables. The final course was a second type of light, clear soup.

During the meal, Ayame gave me further lessons in Japanese dining etiquette. She showed me how to hold chopsticks and explained that I should never stick them into my rice so they stood up. "That reminds people of how incense is placed in sand during a funeral." She also explained why passing morsels of food from one person's chopsticks to another's is considered to be in very bad taste: this was how the bones of the dead were handled after cremation. And there was more: never pick up anything with the thick ends of the chopsticks if you can help it; never put your chopsticks down so they are pointing at someone; and finally, never stab food through with a chopstick. This last rule disappointed me. In the past, it was the only way I could guarantee any food would make it from the plate to my mouth.

I also found out that my habit of dunking pieces of *nigiri* sushi rice-side down in the bowl of soya sauce was considered bad manners. Ayame explained that rice would suck up too much sauce this way—it was thought to be a bit greedy—and also might let grains of rice drop into the soya sauce.

But perhaps the rule that fascinated me the most was about pouring drinks for one another. When the saki bottle was brought to the table, Ayame poured some for me, and then some for her parents. She did not fill her glass, so I assumed she was not going to drink. But then her father took the little bottle and poured some into the small ceramic glass in front of his daughter. A little later, Ayame's mother refilled everyone's cup, but not her own. This time Ayame took the bottle and gave her mother some more saki. By the third time the drinks were being replenished in this way, I looked over at Ayame and raised my eyebrows.

"Ah, so you've noticed," she said. "The Japanese consider it an important part of hospitality to keep their guests' glasses full, but it is thought to be impolite to fill your own. Instead, you must wait for others to notice that your glass is empty so they can fill it for you." I thought of Annisha and Adam and the dinners we used to share. Annisha would have become very parched if she had to wait for me to notice her empty glass.

After dinner, Ayame suggested we take a stroll through the neighborhood. The streets were dry, but a sultry humidity hung in the air.

"Thanks for explaining the dining etiquette," I said as we walked down the cobbled street. "If I had more time here, I might eventually get the knack." Julian's itinerary noted that I would be flying out the day after tomorrow, for Mexico. I had thought at first about seeing if I could book an earlier flight, but with all of Ayame's kind attention, a request like that now seemed a little rude.

"I was happy to do it. I'm quite fascinated, actually, about these little codes of behavior. As Julian may have told you, I have traveled quite extensively, and I always pay attention, in every place I go, to all the unspoken customs, the shared understanding of how things should be done."

"You are clearly more observant than I am," I said. "The only thing I noticed in Istanbul was that Ahmet never touched any-thing with his left hand."

"In many countries, one particular hand is used only for any kind of dirty work. So you would not touch food or another person with that hand."

That was probably it, I thought.

"The interesting thing," said Ayame, "is that the rules we have been raised with seem natural, obvious, logical even. It is not until we start seeing our behavior through the eyes of another culture that we begin to question it or to wonder.

"For example," she continued, "I have read that the tradi-tion of shaking hands originated as a way of showing someone that you were holding no weapons, and so intended no harm or injury to the one you greeted. So why today do I walk into a conference in New York and put out my hand? Do I really mean to show that I'm not carrying a dagger?"

That made me laugh.

"But how some customs start is really not so important. The importance of etiquette, manners, rules, is to make it easier for us to interact with one another. Our shared behaviors make us comfortable; they are ways to show respect to one another. They are all about how we make one another feel. Our daily behaviors broadcast our deepest beliefs."

"But sometimes it gets confusing," I said. "Take opening the door for a woman. There was a time when no gentleman would walk through a door in front of a woman. You had to hold the door open for her and pass through only after she had gone. But I'm not so sure I'm supposed to do that now."

"Yes, that is one of the rules that are changing in the West," said Ayame. "It *was* meant as a sign of respect, was it not? But then some women began to feel that this habit was patronizing, that it suggested they were weak, that they needed help with something as simple as a door. Suddenly, it is unclear whether this custom is polite or not."

"I usually just try to hold doors open for everyone now," I said. "So I don't single women out."

"That is one solution," said Ayame. "Actually, the last time I was in Los Angeles, I noticed that sometimes men held doors for women and sometimes women held doors for men, or other women. It seems as if many people have rethought the etiquette of door-holding."

We had circled around the neighborhood now for a half an hour. The streets looked pretty in the dark—lights shining through rice-paper screens on the windows of some houses, golden lanterns hanging outside others, the moon glittering off the glazed tiled roofs of a few buildings.

We turned down a small lane, and I realized that we had entered the far end of Ayame's street. I was exhausted, but not entirely sure that I would be able to sleep. Nevertheless, I was looking forward to returning to my peaceful room.

As we entered the *ryokan* lobby, Ayame said, "Let me give you Julian's parcel tonight." She led me through the lobby to a door at the far end. I followed her and found myself once again on the wooden veranda, overlooking the garden. A few lamps hung under the eaves, and a small spotlight shone on the bubbling fountain; a few more lights cast bright beams on the statuary. The garden looked otherworldly, magical.

"Please sit," Ayame said, pointing to a small teak bench. "I will be back shortly." Then she disappeared into the inn.

She returned a minute later, holding a small parcel in two hands. It was wrapped in what looked like thick handmade paper and tied with silk cord. She held it out for me, and I carefully took it from her with both hands. Then she looked at me and grinned.

"You know what this letter says, don't you?" I asked.

"Of course," said Ayame, laughing.

When I got back to my room, I untied the package and unfolded the thick mottled paper. Inside was a note, along with a tiny golden crane. I stood the crane up in the palm of my hand and looked at it. The long, gentle curve of its back, its tilted head, its delicate beak. I closed my hand around it and then took the leather sack from around my neck. After I dropped the crane inside, I unfolded the note and read it.

### Live with Kindness

*It is important to remember that just as our words are our thoughts verbalized, so our deeds are our beliefs actualized. No action, no matter how small, is insignificant—how we treat someone defines how we treat everyone, including ourselves. If we disrespect another, we disrespect ourselves. If we are mistrustful of others, we are distrustful of ourselves. If we are cruel to another, we will be cruel to ourselves. If we can't appreciate those around us, we won't appreciate ourselves. With every person we engage, in everything we do, we must be kinder than expected, more generous than anticipated, more positive than we thought possible. Every moment in front of another human being is an opportunity to express our highest values and to influence someone with our humanity. We can make the world better, one person at a time.*

There was no doubt why Julian had made Ayame the safe-keeper of this talisman. Yes, I thought to myself, smiling.

The past twenty-four hours had been a roller coaster for me. The day had started badly in Paris—or at least I had started badly. Whining, sulking, fussing. I had continued on that track right through my arrival in Osaka, my train ride to Kyoto. But all the complaining had not made me feel one bit better. Taking out my frustrations on others hadn't eased my burden one bit. Instead, it was the kindness of others that had helped me. Their decency and gentleness had softened me. And somehow, that had made me easier on myself as well. Julian had written some wise words. But Ayame—Ayame seemed to be living them.

## Chapter Six

THE "ITINERARY" THAT JULIAN had sent me didn't cover the full trip, and it gave no indication of when my travels would end. Instead, it simply listed the next two destinations. As I looked at the dates, I inhaled sharply. Julian didn't seem to be moving me from safekeeper to safekeeper with particular speed.

"Don't worry," said Ayame gently. "To go too quickly on a journey like this would not be good for your health. You need to be able to get a little sleep, a little exercise at each place you stop. I am sure that Julian has arranged the trip like this thinking of your needs, not his."

Once again, Ayame was making me look at things differently. She seemed to move through the world with great gentleness. It was how she responded and how she expected other people to respond—to everyone and everything. She was probably right. Julian was thinking of me. But I wasn't thinking of him. I was impatient to get back because of my own needs. I wasn't worrying about why, or how urgently, he needed these talismans. If Julian felt he could take the time that this itinerary suggested, then I could, too.

THE NEXT DAY Ayame took me to the Kiyomizu Shrine and the Ryoanji Temple, and in the evening we strolled through the Gion district, where geishas still step through the streets on their way to appointments. By the time I crawled into my futon that night, I was feeling a great deal of gratitude to Julian and his itinerary. Tomorrow I would be heading to Oxkutzcab, Mexico, to meet a fellow named Chava Ucan. I had been to Mexico once before—to Acapulco with Annisha—but never to Mérida, where I would be landing, or anywhere else on the Yucatán Peninsula. It occurred to me that this would be a hot time of year to visit Mexico.

"See?" Ayame said the following morning, as she shook my hand in Osaka's Itami airport. "No dagger!" Then we bowed to each other. When Ayame straightened up, a look of concern creased her face.

"Jonathan," she said. "Please try to remember Julian's note. The way you relate to others reveals the way you relate to yourself. You are a good man, but I think you do not always treat yourself that way."

CHAVA UCAN'S WIFE, Sikina, had said she would let me sleep for as long as I could. I wasn't hopeful, but now here I was, opening my eyes to the Mexican sun blaring full force through the bedroom window, the heat sitting on my chest so heavily that I knew morning was long gone.

In our two days together, I hadn't told Ayame much about my life. But she seemed to intuit many things. Now, lying on my bed in Chava's house, the heat rising from the terra cotta floor and radiating from the walls, I was thinking about the way I had treated others in my life. I wasn't proud of my outburst at the Osaka airport. Or about the times I had been short-tempered with a bank teller or a grocery store clerk. And then there were my impatient moments with Adam, and my angry words with Annisha. They were much more frequent than my lack of civility to strangers. Why is it that often we allow ourselves to treat family in ways we wouldn't treat friends—or even those we don't know? Probably because we assume they will forgive us. But that's no excuse. I was making resolutions to change the way I behaved to everyone in my life. But there were some things that I just wouldn't be able to make up for. Like the way I treated Juan.

THE FIRST SUGGESTION I got that things might not be going well for Juan at work was the lunch meeting I had with David and his boss, Sven, shortly after I had left the lab.

Sven asked me what I thought of my former supervisor. I started to praise his leadership, when Sven held up his hand.

"No, no, not as a boss. I know he's a nice guy. I mean his vision. His technical knowledge. Is he on his game? Is he cutting edge?

Are we being as progressive, as aggressive, in development as we could be?"

It was an awkward conversation. Every time I said something positive about Juan, David and Sven frowned, as if I'd given the wrong answer. Eventually I just stopped speaking.

"Listen," said David, "I'm not saying Juan isn't a bright guy. And I'm sure that at one point he was a leader in his field. But I'm just thinking that there are younger minds out there, a whole new generation of engineers and hardware designers who may be thinking outside the box. Who may have a fresh approach."

Younger, right. I suspected that what David was really saying was "cheaper." David was always looking for a way to make the bottom line look a little better.

When the waitress came by to clear the table, my plate was still full. And I was feeling queasy. I knew that Juan had the most brilliant, innovative engineering mind I had ever encountered. What's more, he was a genius at getting his people to look at things in new ways, to be creative both in problem-solving and in technical advances. But Sven and David were having none of that. They seemed to have made up their minds, and everything I said to contradict them was taking me down a notch in their estimation. It was clear that if I wanted to secure my own career, I would have to back off protecting Juan's. Now, thousands of miles away from my office, I could see that in one moment at lunch, I had made a cowardly decision which ended up costing both of us in the gravest way possible.

I HAD WOKEN UP in Mexico thinking of that lunch scene. The truth was, however, that it had first entered my mind when I read the "kindness" note—and I was pushing it out of my thoughts during the whole of my long trip from Osaka to Mérida. The journey had taken more than twenty-four hours, with connections in Tokyo, Los Angeles and Mexico City. During all of that, I had tried to embrace Ayame's peacefulness and ease. And I'd forced myself to stop worrying about time. I napped here and there, and gave myself over to jet lag and disorientation. I looked at my phone as little as possible. Landing in Mérida at the close of what was, according to the calendar, the same day that I had left Japan, I was overcome with a peculiar sense of nonchalance. So when a middle-aged woman reached for my elbow as I exited the airport doors, I didn't start.

Sikina Ucan apologized for her husband's absence.

"He has to wake up very early tomorrow to get to work. I told him I would get you. We both thought that you would need to sleep for a while tomorrow morning, so Chava will get a ride to the site from a friend, and then I will bring you there in the afternoon to say hello."

On the long, dark ride from Mérida to Oxkutzcab, Sikina told me that Chava was a field technician working with a team that was excavating Mayan ruins outside of Oxkutzcab.

"He is very excited about giving you a tour of the archaeological dig and telling you a bit about his work. Sikina talked a little more about Chava, herself and her children. She told me that she and Chava had met Julian several years ago when he was touring through the Yucatán, visiting various Mayan ruins and studying the culture.

"What a wonderful man," Sikina said, tucking a piece of her long dark hair behind her ear. "So wise . . . and so fun." But she said nothing about the talisman or the reason for my visit.

I was beginning to appreciate that Julian had chosen each safekeeper carefully. Each seemed to have a certain relationship with the talisman and its wisdom. According to Sikina, Chava wanted to share some of his life with me. And while I might have asked for the talisman right away, I decided to see if I could figure out what the note would say, what lesson I might learn from Chava. By the time we got to Oxkutzcab, it was around one in the morning. Sikina pulled the truck up in front of a small pale pink stuccoed house. Inside she pointed to a door to one side of the kitchen-living area.

The bedroom was tiny, but neat. I dropped my luggage onto the floor and collapsed on the bed. I was asleep before I even got my clothes off.

IT WAS PROBABLY THE HEAT that woke me up, but it was the smell of something rich and savory that drew me out of the bedroom and into the kitchen.

"Oh, good," said Sikina, wiping her hands on her apron. "I was hoping that lunch might get you up. We should head out soon."

Sikina motioned for me to sit down at the small table tucked into a corner of her cramped kitchen. The table was painted bright yellow, and each of the four chairs was a different color. Annisha would love this, I thought. I pulled the turquoise chair out and sat down, as Sikina placed a steaming plate in front of me.

"*Codzitos,*" she said. "Little tacos, with meat and tomato sauce. And guava juice," she added, pointing to a tall blue glass in front of me.

The food was delicious, and I was regretting how much I

had put away as I climbed into Sikina's truck an hour later. I had washed up and changed my clothes, but I was still feeling distressingly full.

The truck lurched forward as Sikina put it into gear. She looked over at my ashen face and smiled.

"Okay," she said. "I will give you a short tour of our town so your stomach can rest before we get out on the highway."

Sikina drove slowly through the streets of Oxkutzcab. We moved through neighborhoods of low square houses, some white-washed, others painted in fanciful shades, and still others built of unadorned cement blocks. The flat roofs were of tin or tile, but there were also a number of small brightly painted oval-shaped houses with peaked thatched roofs.

"That is a traditional Mayan hut," said Sikina, pointing to one.

The residential streets had a wonderfully irregular look to them. Low stone or concrete walls bordered front yards that were sometimes dry, empty-looking spaces—sometimes overgrown riots of palm trees, hibiscus, and all sorts of plants and bushes I didn't recognize. Fancy cast-iron railings and gates alternated with lines of laundry flapping in the breeze. In the village center were several churches, small restaurants and hotels, and other buildings painted in bright shades of terra cotta or blue or yellow. The streets were dusty and relatively quiet: few cars, but a number of bikes, motorcycles, pedestrians and food carts making their way slowly through the heat.

As we drove along the narrow asphalt road, the houses and buildings gave way to more and more trees and shrubs until the town was behind us and low rolling hills stretched across the horizon. "Puuc Hills," Sikina told me. "They are full of Mayan ruins, big and small. Tomorrow Chava wants to take you to Uxmal. That was once a city of more than 20,000. But today we go to a smaller, more forgotten place."

Half an hour after we had set off, we turned down a rough dirt road that seemed to follow a small valley. We bounced down it for some way, the thick forest rising up on either side of us until we passed under a wooden arch with a name carved across it. Eventually we pulled up in an open space. There were many people buzzing about, including what appeared to be a school group heading into a low, modern-looking building. I could see an assortment of thatched Mayan huts, but even they looked relatively new and very much in use. This is not what I had expected from an archaeological site.

"Oh, there is a lot more going on here," said Sikina when I commented. "This is also a nature preserve and a research facility. It is over four thousand acres."

We had not been out of the truck for more than a few minutes when a short, squarish man in a ball cap, shorts and heavy boots came loping toward us.

"*Hola,* Jonathan!" he said.

I smiled and extended my hand. Chava pumped it vigorously.

"*Bix a beel?* How are you?"

You only had to talk with Chava for a minute to realize that his passion was history. He did ask about my trip, about Julian, about whether Sikina had fed me sufficiently. But his voice did not become fully alive until he started to talk about the place where he was working. Sikina stayed back at one of the offices, visiting friends who worked at the nature preserve. As Chava led me past the open area and through the forested hillside, he explained the current focus of the excavations at this location.

I wondered what, if anything, this had to do with the talisman, and whether I really needed a tour, but I was beginning to see that this trip was going to have a rhythm of its own that I could do very little to change.

"Archaeologists have worked here off and on for decades," Chava told me as we pushed our way through the foliage, "but it's only in past few years or so that we've begun to realize that this site may offer us some new clues about the collapse of the Mayan Empire."

It was as if my father had been reborn in this middle-aged Mayan archaeologist. I found myself smiling as Chava continued his running commentary.

The people speaking the Mayan language had, he said, appeared in the Yucatán well over four thousand years ago. For the next three thousand years, sophisticated, very densely populated cities sprang up throughout the Mayan world. At the height of the Mayan period, most of the land between these city-states was covered with farms and villages. And all the major centers were connected with white limestone roads.

The city-states not only operated under elaborate political systems but were marvels of architecture as well: stepped pyramids and temples, multiple-story dwellings, ornate courtyards and public squares. The Maya, Chava said, also created breathtaking art works and developed one of the world's earliest writing systems. And their sophisticated math skills allowed them to make great advances in astronomy, which led to perhaps their most famous achievement: the Mayan calendar. Chava's thoughts were spilling out like a finely crafted lecture, but they also seemed threaded with personal pride, as if he were talking about people he knew and loved.

But then somewhere between 900 and 1000 AD, Chava explained, six hundred years before the arrival of the Spanish, the civilization began to crumble. Over the next two hundred years or so, he told me, a sadness edging his words, 90 percent of the population disappeared, the cities were abandoned, and the greatness of the Mayan world became a memory. It took only a century or two for the forests to take over the cities, for green growth to mask the monuments and roadways, for the remaining population to scatter across the countryside, clinging to tiny villages and subsistence agriculture. These survivors, Chava noted, were his ancestors.

As he talked, Chava led me through the forest, over tree roots and crumbling stones. Along the way, I spotted the occasional fieldworker moving along the paths, but the place was hardly quiet or empty. Birds squawked and sang out as they swooped through the trees. I heard branches rustling and scurrying sounds all around us. I tried to concentrate on the birds and not think of spiders, scorpions or pumas. Chava stopped now and then to point out barely revealed formations of stones or freshly excavated sites. He had walked me around a small pyramid. It was stepped, like the pictures I had seen of the famous pyramid at Chichen Itza but was only about thirty-five feet high. And then we arrived in front of what looked to be the remains of buildings laid out around two sides of large raised stone. The bottoms of the walls were composed of stone squares, and the tops were covered with what looked like a stone-column motif. "A half-finished palace here," said Chava. "Around a plaza, a public space."

I walked around the base of the ruins and peered at the stone building blocks.

"You said they didn't have metal tools?"

"That's right," said Chava. "Just granite, flint, obsidian. There aren't materials to make metal in these parts."

I ran my hand across the foundation. "Incredible."

"Shall we take a short rest?" Chava asked, moving to the edge of the raised stone plaza and sitting down. He pulled a water bottle from the pack he had been carrying and handed it to me. I walked over and took it from him gratefully. The trees provided shade, but the heat seemed to rise from the forest floor as well as pounding down from above the tree-tops. My shirt was clinging to my back; my pants were glued to my legs.

"That's what I like about this work, you know," Chava said. "The mysteries. We know that some of the abandoned cities we see were simply left by people moving about. But the population didn't just move—it disappeared. And even the remaining populations did not stay on in the big cities."

Chava went on to explain that scientists who studied Mayan skeletons had said that the bones, even the bones of the royalty, suggested that in the later years of the civilization, food was scarce. That might have been the result of overhunting. Another possibility was a plague of pests or some sort of agricultural disaster, perhaps caused by deforestation. But the most likely cause of the food shortage was an extended drought. "There isn't much water in Yucatán at the best of times," he laughed. And of course, disease, wars or other violence could have decimated the population as well.

Chava stood up and put the water bottle back in his pack.

"But here, at this site," he said, "we see something we don't often see at the excavations. Come." Chava led me to one side of the ruins. The main exterior featured square archways supported by short, round columns. But Chava was looking at the ground in front of the building.

"Now," said Chava, pointing at an assembly of stones laid out on the ground. It wasn't a neat formation, but it didn't look haphazard either. "What would you guess that was?"

"I don't know," I said, moving closer. There were small tufts of grass between the stones. A lizard scurried across one corner and disappeared down the side of the pile. "Is it the beginning of a building? Or something that fell down?"

"That, my friend," said Chava, "is a wall. Not a wall that has fallen down, but one that was assembled ahead of time and laid here, waiting to be moved up there to make a second story. It was all ready to go, but the work was not finished. This is something you don't see in a site that was abandoned because of long drought or disease. This work wasn't stopped—it was *interrupted*."

When we had started this little tour, it all felt a bit random—taking a crash course in archaeology, becoming immersed in the working world of someone I just met. But I was beginning to see why Chava might want to show all this to everyone he encountered, why he might want to share his work with a stranger, why a job like his might hook a person. There were so many questions to be answered.

"What do you think it was?" I asked. "Were they attacked or something?"

"War or violence seems likely here, doesn't it?" said Chava. "We have found a quantity of spearheads. But no burned buildings or walls or barricades for defense. And if it was an unexpected attack, well . . . you need to see another thing." Chava gestured for me to come away from the wall. "Can you take just a bit more climbing?"

Chava led the way, up a winding, twisting path. Here and there were the remains of crumbling stairs, which we scrambled over. Chava stopped climbing near the top of the hill and headed over to a flat area of stakes and stones. It was obvious that an excavation was under way. Cleared from the undergrowth were the stone bases of walls surrounding dry dirt pits. In one, a young blond woman squatted in a corner, carefully sweeping dirt away from a buried object with a small brush. In another corner of the pit were various bits of rock and broken pottery with numbered flags and labels on them.

"Jonathan," said Chava as the woman stood up. "This is Ellen. Ellen, this is Jonathan."

Ellen was another field technician, working with a team from an American university.

"I was just explaining to Jonathan about the recent discoveries. Maybe you could tell him about these hilltop homes," said Chava. Ellen nodded and wiped her brow with a scarf she took from the pocket of her pants. Like Chava, she seemed to need no encouragement to talk about her work.

She explained that what I was looking at were the remains of meal preparation. The grinding stone for the corn had been rested against the doorframe, but not put away. The neatly laid-out pots suggested that work had started but then stopped midway through. Everything had been left the way people would leave things if they thought they would be returning shortly. They left quickly, but they did not appear to have run off in terror. Everything was orderly, and there were no signs of chaos or attack.

"Ah," sighed Chava. "We have a lot of work to do before we solve these mysteries."

"Speaking of which," said Ellen. "I hope you'll excuse me while I get back to it. I want to get a bit more done before I leave for the day."

Chava and I stood on the hilltop for a few minutes more, gazing over the canopy of trees. I looked back at Ellen crouched in the dirt. There was less shade up here, and although the sun was not as high in the sky as it had been when I first arrived, it was still hot.

"That's one thing I don't get," I said to Chava.

Chava cocked his head.

"The work," I said. "The digging. It seems to move so slowly. I thought electrical engineering and technical design were painstaking, but this. . ." I waved my hand in Ellen's direction. "This moves by fractions of inches. How do you manage?"

"Ah yes, I know," said Chava, smiling. "You can work all day, and at the end of it, what have you done? Moved a few pounds of sand, right?"

I shrugged my shoulders.

"It's easy to make light of the work we do. The American fieldworkers sometimes refer to themselves as 'shovelbums.' But we all have to keep reminding ourselves that we can't rush our work, that we must be patient. And above all, we must work carefully, accurately, with the greatest professionalism, even if we are feeling bored or restless. It's so easy to destroy important artifacts or miss things altogether."

Chava began to head back toward the rough stairs. He looked over his shoulder at me.

"Each carefully excavated square may seem small, Jonathan,

but together, all these little plots can add up to an important historical discovery, a real advance in knowledge. I like to think that if we 'shovelbums' do our work well, our small contributions can add up to something really important. We can actually solve great mysteries."

On the way home, Sikina insisted that I sit next to the window in the truck while she squeezed herself between Chava and me. I kept the window rolled all the way down, and occasionally stuck my head out like a goofy golden retriever. The dry rushing air felt wonderful. Once we were winding our way through the house-lined streets of Oxkutzcab, there was another reason to keep my head leaning out the window—the seductive smell of cooking. I realized how ravenous I was, but it also dawned on me that, since we had all been out all day, it was unlikely supper would be waiting on the stove when we got back.

"I'm just thinking," I said to Chava and Sikina, "why don't I take you two out for dinner in town? You've spent so much of your day entertaining me."

"Oh no," said Sikina. "We can't do that. Zama is waiting for us."

It turned out that we were heading to the home of Chava and Sikina's married daughter. She and her husband had prepared a big dinner for us.

It was a crowded, noisy evening. As well as Zama and her husband and their three small children, various neighbors dropped in to say hi. Music played, my glass was filled and refilled, and my plate was piled high. As the children chased one another around the backyard, my eyes followed Zama's six-year-old son, Eme. He was a bit smaller than Adam, but with his bubbly laugh and the way his body was constantly in motion, even when he sat down, Eme reminded me of my son. After I'd finished eating, I walked through the house and out onto the dirt street, where it was a little more quiet. I tried to phone home, but my cell reception had been spotty since I landed in Mexico, and I couldn't get through. I composed a message to Adam.

*Hey buddy,* I wrote. *I am seeing the most amazing things here. When I have more time I will tell you all about them. But right now, I just wanted to say that I love you.*

The message would get sent out whenever my phone got reception. In the meantime, I would go back to the party, but my heart was no longer in it.

Chava seemed to notice how quiet I had become after my return, and about thirty minutes later he suggested we depart. By the time I was lying in my bed later that night, having written in my journal about watching Chava's happy family, my chest was tight from longing. I wanted nothing more than to have my son sprawled next to me. How had I not treasured those moments when they were so easily in reach?

THE NEXT MORNING, Chava and I picked our way through the car park in the predawn darkness. I had toyed with the thought of asking Sikina to take me back to the airport in Mérida instead, to see if I could get an earlier flight out of Mexico, but Ayame's words returned to me. Julian seemed to be pacing this trip with a reason. What's more, Chava seemed intent on continuing my Mayan education, and I would have felt bad suggesting that we cut it short. He had insisted that we come out here, to Uxmal, before daybreak.

"When the sun comes up," he had said, "the people appear. You want to see this alone, or almost alone."

Chava had many connections with the people who ran the site, so a security guard had been instructed to meet us at the entrance to the building that acted as the gateway to the temples and the ruins. We could see his uniformed figure silhouetted against the museum's front door.

When we approached, he and Chava exchanged a few words in Maya, and the guard opened the door for us. Then he pointed across the lobby and said something else.

"I know the way," said Chava. "Just follow me."

Ten minutes later we were standing outside. In the dim light, a magnificent pyramid rose before us over a hundred feet high and at least two hundred feet wide. Unlike the small pyramid I had seen yesterday, or the pictures I had seen of other Mayan pyramids, this one seemed to have an oval base. "Temple of the Magician," said Chava.

While we stood, the sun climbed behind us. As it did, its light hit the stones of the temple, making them glow golden, as if an enormous fire had been lit inside the pyramid.

Chava leaned sideways toward me and said in a low voice, "Amazing, no? To think that men built this. Ordinary men like you and me, capable of such accomplishments, such excellence." I nodded, dumbstruck by what was before me.

We watched the pyramid as the sky lightened around it. Then Chava started walking. He was heading toward the structure.

"Tourists are no longer allowed to walk up the steps, but we have special permission." Instead of starting up the steps directly in front of us, Chava walked around the base. The thought of scaling the pyramid excited me. I was suddenly glad that Chava was taking my education so seriously.

"The other side is better for climbing," he explained as he

led me around to the opposite face of the pyramid.

As I stood at the bottom of the pyramid, the stone rising high above me, the staggering height became clear. It would be a tough climb. Chava started up, and I followed. We made our way slowly up the smooth, hard steps. They were steep and narrow, and the sensation of moving up an enormous open staircase was disorienting. Chava told me that many of the pyramids have metal chains to hang on to as you climb. I could see why. By the time we reached the very top, I was sweating like I'd just finished a marathon.

"This is the best view of Uxmal," said Chava. "Sit, rest, look."

Chava dropped his small canvas backpack to the ground and squatted down onto his heels. I did the same.

The Uxmal site stretched around us for hundreds of acres. Much of the remains of the ancient city were still covered in vegetation. The only suggestion of many of the streets and buildings were flat stretches broken by squarish mounds. Directly below us, however, was a series of vast stone ruins.

Chava told me that when Uxmal was inhabited, the houses would have stretched out for many more acres than what I now saw before me. He pointed out another pyramid, half-covered with vegetation, that was called the Great Pyramid, and he told me about the other ruined buildings that we could see all around us.

"Have you ever heard the legend of this pyramid?" Chava asked me after describing the city at our feet. I shook my head.

"There are many different versions of the tale," said Chava.

The legend that Chava recounted described how, long ago, the king of Uxmal was warned that when a certain gong in the city was struck, his empire would fall to a man not born of woman. One day, indeed, the gong sounded, and the king was dismayed to discover that the person who had struck it was a dwarf boy hatched from an egg by an old, childless woman. The king summoned the dwarf to his palace and was going to execute him, when he had a change of heart. Instead of killing the boy on the spot, he decided to set the dwarf an impossible task. If the dwarf could build the king a magnificent temple, taller than any other building in the city and could do this in one single night, his life would be saved.

When the king awoke the next morning, he was astonished to see towering before him a majestic pyramid. The dwarf's life was spared, and the pyramid became known as the Temple of the Magician.

"In some versions of the story, the dwarf himself is created by the old woman overnight. In others, he is set many feats of strength and tests, including the building of the pyramid. But what each version has in common," said Chava, "is the idea that this extraordinary structure was created in the space of just one night."

Chava took two water bottles out of his pack. He passed one to me and took a swig out of the other, then wiped his mouth with the back of his hand.

"Perhaps it's because of the work I do," he continued, "but that story delights me. It tells us so much about our dreams, our desires. What does the king wish for? No, it's not so much that he wants a great temple. He could have had his subjects build him that at any time. What he wants is for this remarkable creation to happen overnight!"

"I guess nothing changes," I said with a laugh. "Everyone wants everything in a hurry."

"Yes, exactly," said Chava. "But that is just not possible, is it? After all, the accomplishment of the king's task proves that the dwarf is, in fact, a magician. It is not in the power of a mere human to make something truly marvelous in an instant. People need patience. People need to build things slowly, one brick at a time. As much as we would love to achieve great things quickly, it is not the way our world works. Genius is a process."

Chava had placed his canvas knapsack on his lap and was digging around inside. After a few seconds, he pulled out a small cloth bag and handed it to me.

"Shall I open this now?" I asked. Chava nodded.

The top of the red woven bag was tied with a bit of string. I worked at the knot until it fell open, and then lifted the bag and emptied its contents onto my lap. There was a note and a tiny red clay object. I picked it up and looked at it. It appeared to be a miniature model of a pyramid.

I unfolded the piece of paper and read the words on it.

*Make Small Daily Progress*
*The way we do small things determines the way that we do everything. If we execute our minor tasks well, we will also excel at our larger efforts. Mastery then becomes our way of being. But more than this—each tiny effort builds on the next, so that brick by brick, magnificent things can be created, great confidence grows and uncommon dreams are realized. The truly wise recognize that small daily improvements always lead to exceptional results over time.*

The sun was considerably higher in the sky than it had been at the start of our climb. Its heat was beginning to press down on me. I lifted the corner of my shirt and wiped some perspiration from my brow.

Chava looked over and immediately began to stand up.

"I'm sorry for keeping you so long up here," he said. "I know you are not used to the temperatures. Let's head out. On the way down, I want to show you one more thing."

We began our descent, which I found more difficult than the climb up. Walking down the steep, narrow steps, facing out across the plaza, made me realize the heights I'd scaled and the absence of anything that might prevent me from slipping and crashing down these smooth stone steps. I was relieved when Chava signaled me to stop lowering myself and instead move along sideways. Chava was ahead of me, but eventually he stopped in front of a large arched doorway that opened along one side of the pyramid.

"This," Chava said, with a flourish of his hand toward the doorway, "is the irony of that legend, as far as I'm concerned."

"Really?" I said.

"This pyramid was supposed to have been built overnight, but nothing could be further from the truth," said Chava. "Instead, it was built over hundreds of years. In fact, it was rebuilt again and again. Five times! And each time the new pyramid was constructed on top of the old. My ancestors thought this imbued the temple with all the accumulated power and greatness of its predecessor. This doorway is just a remnant of one of the earlier pyramids that was here. What you see around it was added on later."

"Wow," I said. I was looking up at the carvings of mystical creatures, or perhaps Mayan gods, that ran along the door frame. It was intricate, detailed artistry. It would indeed have been magic if anything like this happened in months, never mind overnight.

"Yesterday I was telling you that I hope my work will uncover clues about the end of the Mayan Empire," said Chava. "But the beginnings are what really interest me—how all this came to be. You talk about an archaeological dig being painstaking work, but the creation of a civilization, the building of vast cities, these pyramids here—*that* is slow, painstaking work."

I nodded, and we were both quiet for a minute.

"It is good to remember that," Chava said quietly. "That every big dream starts small."

It was Chava who took me to the airport in Mérida the next day. The drive was almost two hours long, and after chatting amiably for the first half-hour we fell silent. I took out my phone, but I still couldn't get a signal. I started to scroll through some of my pictures. I paused over a shot of Adam in his soccer uniform, his foot resting uncertainly on a ball.

Chava glanced over. "You are feeling a bit homesick," he said.

"Yeah," I said.

"You are on your way home, Jonathan," he replied after a moment. "You are on your way home."

We had passed through the small town of Ticul, past scruffy farmland and rocky pastures. We sat without talking for a little longer before I pulled my journal from my backpack and took out the most recent note. I had been writing my reflections about the journey, the talismans and the letters in the journal, as Julian had asked. I wasn't entirely sure what I thought of this most recent message.

Eventually Chava looked toward the notebook on my lap and said, "Jonathan, did Sikina tell you about our son, Avali?"

"Just that he lives in Mexico City, and she misses him," I replied.

That made Chava laugh loudly. I looked at him quizzically.

"Sorry," said Chava, "I can't believe she stopped there. Avali is a doctor. Sikina is very proud of him. Usually, that's one of the first things she tells people."

"I can understand," I said, "why she would be proud."

There was a beat of silence and then Chava continued.

"When Avali was eight years old he came to me and said, 'Papa, I want to become a doctor and help sick people. How do I do it?' Now, Jonathan, what could I say? Sikina and I, neither one of us went to university. Most of my family hadn't got past elementary school. And not just that. None of us had ever left Yucatán. I had no idea how someone would become a doctor. But there was little Avali, with all the hope of a child, and I realized that I did know one thing. I pulled him on my lap, and I said, 'Son, this is how you begin. Tomorrow, you go to school, and you listen to everything the teacher says. And you work harder than you have ever worked. And then you come home and tell me what you've learned.'"

Chava was smiling softly, as if he could see his young son in front of him. He nodded his head slightly, and then continued.

"So he began. Each test, each assignment, I told him, 'Do well on this, and you are on your way to becoming a doctor.' None of us knew the road ahead, so we just concentrated on the step before us. As he got older, we talked to everyone we knew—the archaeologists and researchers at the sites I was working on, the nurses and doctors at the hospital, even tourists we met at the ruins or in town. Slowly but surely, Avali,

Sikina and I figured out the next steps. Before we knew it, Avali was graduating from university in Mexico City."

"Small daily improvements can lead to great things, right?" I said.

"The tiniest of actions is always better than the boldest of intentions," said Chava. "And results always speak louder than words."

Like the other safekeepers, Chava clearly understood, and *lived*, the wisdom of the talisman he had guarded. He saw it in his job, he saw it with his son. But how would it look in my life? I wasn't sure what precious achievement I should be striving for, what accomplishments—and dreams—I should be taking my small steps toward. I used to think it was that CEO job, or the enormous house, or even a Ferrari, like Julian had. But now, I wasn't sure. It was not until we reached the airport that I scribbled something in the journal. *Push-ups,* I wrote. I would start the day tomorrow with twenty push-ups. I would go from there.

I FOUND IT SURPRISINGLY hard to say good-bye to Chava. He and Sikina had reminded me so much of my parents. And I found myself wanting to spend more time with his family. Perhaps if I had been going home, I wouldn't have felt that way. But I was heading again into the unknown—Barcelona this time. In the airport, I managed to get a signal. I phoned Annisha, but I got her voicemail. I decided to write Adam and Annisha another note, telling them about my Mexican stay, but when I opened my inbox, I noticed a message from Tessa. That was odd. We weren't working on anything together.

*Hi Jonathan,* it started.

*I was talking to Nawang today, asking when you'd be back. She said she didn't know. She thinks that you may not return at all. I couldn't believe how much that upset me. And that got me thinking. I don't know quite how to say this, so I'm just going to plunge right in. The rumor around the office is that you are in the process of getting a divorce. Maybe it's too soon for you, but I have always felt there was something between us. If you don't come back to work here, I wouldn't want to think that we'd missed an opportunity to get together. I think that we might be good for each other. Anyhow, I'm babbling. Just wanted to let you know that I'm thinking about you.*

*Tessa*

# CHAPTER SEVEN

WHEN I WAS FIVE, my father took me to my first basketball game. It wasn't the NBA, but it was the most exciting game I have ever seen.

It was the elementary school semifinals, held at Parkview Public School, where my father taught sixth grade. I had been there the previous summer, when my dad set up his classroom for the first day of school. My sister and I colored on scrap paper while Dad put up posters of animals and strange people. The posters all had writing on them, and I had no idea what they were about. But it was clear to me that my father must be truly brilliant to teach math, and reading, and everything else to boys and girls of the advanced age of eleven.

This basketball game, however, was the first indication that my father had skills and responsibilities which transcended his classroom gifts. I sat on the end of a long wooden bench in an enormous gym. Boys who looked old and big enough to be adults—in my eyes, at least—stretched down the length of the seat. My father was talking to them, giving instructions. And each of those boys had his eyes on my father—absorbing every word he said as if he were sharing with them the secrets of the universe.

I don't remember any of the game. The only thing that has stuck with me is the way my chest swelled each time my dad talked to his team, and each time he looked over at me and smiled.

By fourth grade, however, that game was in the distant past, and my pride had been replaced by worry. My teacher that year was Mrs. Higginbottom—a woman who sometimes came to work with a forgotten curler sticking in the back of her hair. She wore such outrageously mismatched clothes that even nine-year-old boys took notice. Mrs. Higginbottom managed to keep control of the class only with the help of Mrs. Dorman, from the classroom next door, and frequent visits from the principal. But even the constant threat of detentions and extra homework couldn't keep us from congregating in the school yard at recess to come up with rude nicknames for her. Mrs. Higginbottom was making it clear to me that teachers were not necessarily figures of respect; that teachers could often be the butt of the joke.

I was pretty certain my father was nothing like Mrs. Higginbottom—that kids didn't copy from each other's tests the moment his back was turned, or try to fool him into thinking he had lost whole assignments that they had never bothered to hand in. But I couldn't stop asking the question: if they let Mrs. Higginbottom be a teacher, what did that say about Dad?

By seventh grade, my kindergarten view of Dad's godlike status had vanished. Now all I could think of was that my father had chosen to spend his life hanging out with *little kids*. My friends' fathers were doctors and lawyers, forklift operators and businessmen. They drove home at the end of the day with expensive briefcases stuffed with files, or white hardhats in the back windows of their trucks. My dad came home with piles of clumsily put together booklets on "Ainshint Egipt" and stacks of worksheets on fractions and decimals.

By high school, I was certain. The reason Dad was an elementary school teacher, the reason he clung to this position, was that he had no ambition—a deficit so marked that he failed to comprehend or acknowledge the embarrassment of his career. I discovered that he had been approached many times to become a vice principal or a principal but had turned down each offer. His line was that he loved the classroom—and if he couldn't teach, he would rather do something else altogether. But *I* knew the truth: Dad was some kind of lazy nut.

By the time I was working full-time myself, I had come to recognize that, of course, Dad was nothing like Mrs. Higginbottom. I could see that he truly loved what he was doing, and that he was good at it. But the question of ambition continued to nag at me.

That's what I was thinking about as Lluis Costa told me his story.

LLUIS HAD MET ME at the Barcelona airport. Like Ahmet, he was holding up a little sign with my name on it. He was probably in his early thirties, but he had a boyish look about him, his dark brown curls cropped close to his head. He was wearing a crisp navy blazer and dark gray slacks. His bright red tie flashed against the whiteness of his shirt.

"*Hola, hola.* Welcome Jonathan," he said. "Lluis Costa at your service. It is a great pleasure to meet a member of Julian's family."

Before I could even respond, Lluis placed his hands on my upper arms, leaned forward and kissed me on both cheeks.

"Now," he said, putting his arm around my shoulders, "let us get to know each other better over a nice dinner and a good bottle of wine."

Lluis's familiarity made me a bit uncomfortable. I had enjoyed the time I spent with Ahmet, Ayame, Chava and Sikina, but I wasn't on a mission to make new friends. I really just wanted to get the talismans. And get home.

Lluis led me out of the terminal and to the taxi stand outside the doors. Instead of heading to the first cab in line, he made a beeline to the last car. Lluis opened the back door with a flourish, sweeping his hand toward the empty seat as if to say, "after you." I didn't move, however. It was clear that the cab was empty. Completely empty.

"Lluis," I said, "There's no driver. The taxi driver isn't in the car."

"No, of course not," said Lluis. "He was meeting you inside. I'm the driver, Jonathan. This is my taxi."

It seemed odd to sit in the backseat when my companion, taxi driver or not, was in the front seat, but Lluis was persistently directing me into the car. Once I was seated, he popped the trunk and put my luggage inside. I could see him waving and calling out to some of the other drivers as he made his way around to the driver's side. Lluis had a joyfulness that you don't often see in cab drivers, or at least not the ones in my town. After he climbed behind the wheel, he turned to me.

"So, Jonathan. Have you been to Barcelona before?"

When I shook my head, Lluis nodded. "Ah, then, you are in luck. You've got the right driver to show you around. But first—you must be tired. I've booked you into a superb hotel in the Eixample district. I will get you there so you can freshen up and rest. And then I'll pick you back up about nine p.m., so we can have dinner on the waterfront. Is that agreeable?'

I had to admit that Lluis was a good driver. He seemed to move in and out of the traffic with ease. The air in the taxi was cool, but not cold. Classical music played softly. I noticed a small caddy over the back of the driver's seat. In it was a box of tissues, a bottle of hand sanitizer and some packages of towelettes. A hanging folder over the back of the passenger seat contained two stacks of colorful flyers. I pulled a flyer out from each stack—a tourist map of Barcelona and a gallery guide. I wondered if all taxis in Barcelona were this well supplied.

As we got into the city center, Lluis began to weave through the narrow streets.

"This may not be the most direct way, but it is the most scenic. I thought you might like to take a look at some of the nineteenth-century architecture in this part of town. It is quite stunning."

Lluis was right. Many of the buildings reminded me of the art nouveau structures of Paris and New York, with their embellished stone facades, cast-iron balconies and long, mullioned windows.

"Wow," I gasped as we passed by an ornate church—all dripping spires and soft crenellation.

"Ah, yes, Antoni Gaudí's Sagrada Família. Barcelona's most renowned architect. Tomorrow, if you are interested, we will come back here. No one should leave Barcelona before getting up close to Gaudí's work."

We continued past the church, turned a corner and then stopped at a red light. When it changed to green, Lluis stepped gently on the gas. We hadn't even reached the center of the intersection when the roar of an accelerating engine made me snap my head around. Another taxi on the cross street was barreling through the red light. It showed no signs of slowing as it raced toward us. I was sure it was about to strike the door right next to my seat. My heart jumped as I dove to the other side and covered my head with my arms. Then I heard squealing tires and the sickening screech of metal against metal. But miraculously *our* car was still moving smoothly, although more slowly now. I raised my head and looked up. Lluis was carefully pulling our taxi over to the side of the street on the other side of the intersection. He had narrowly managed to fly ahead of the speeding car to avoid being hit. After stopping, Lluis put his hazard lights on and then turned to me.

"Are you okay, Jonathan?" he asked.

I nodded. We both looked out the rearview window. The other cab was crushed up into the grill of a car on the opposite side of the cross street. There were skid marks snaking through the center of the intersection where the taxi had obviously slid and twisted after the driver had slammed on the brakes.

Before I could gather my wits about me, Lluis had jumped out of the car and was dashing toward the accident. By the time

I reached the scene, he had helped a stunned-looking woman and a small frightened girl out of the backseat of the other cab. The woman was holding her head, and Lluis was bending down to talk to the child. The driver of the car that the taxi had hit had managed to get his door open and was standing unsteadily on the street. He looked shaken but unharmed.

I leaned into the front passenger window of the stranded cab. The driver was slumped forward, his face resting against the steering wheel. Blood was dripping from his forehead.

The police and an ambulance arrived a few minutes later. By that time, the cab driver had regained consciousness and was trying to tell Lluis what had happened. He seemed very young and very upset. Eventually the paramedics approached and started to check the cabbie's injuries. Lluis and I moved over to the squad car to give our statements to the police. Lluis translated for me, and then we waited for the taxi passenger to explain what she had seen. The paramedics offered to send another ambulance to take the mother to the hospital, to be checked out, but she said she and her daughter felt fine. Once the ambulance had pulled away and all the officials were gone, Lluis approached the woman again, talking softly. Eventually she nodded her head and Lluis turned to me.

"I've convinced her to let me take her to the hospital, just to be on the safe side. I hope you don't mind one more short delay, Jonathan," said Lluis.

"Of course not," I answered.

LLUIS RETURNED TO THE CAB after escorting the woman and her daughter into the emergency ward.

"I'm so sorry you had to start your visit to Barcelona that way, Jonathan," he said.

"Please don't worry about me," I said. I had to admit that the accident had unnerved me, but if Lluis hadn't been my driver it could have been so much worse. I was feeling fortunate, not hard done by.

Twenty minutes later we pulled up to a white stone building with arched windows and cast-iron planters. A liveried bell-man was positioned outside a large brass revolving door. Lluis parked his car in the spot designated for taxis and waved at the bellman before hopping out of the car. I saw him hurry over to open my door but got out of the car first. Lluis pulled my lug-gage from the trunk. As we approached the hotel, the bellman greeted him by name and they exchanged a few words as the bellman opened a heavy glass door next to the revolving one. Once inside the lobby, Lluis waved at a porter who was head-ing toward us and went straight for the concierge desk. A tall, thin man stood behind the desk, reading something. When he looked up and saw Lluis walking toward him, he threw up his hands and called out, *"Bon dia, Lluis!"*

He came out from behind the desk to embrace Lluis before turning to me.

"This is the honored guest I was telling you about. Jonathan Landry, a relative of Julian's," said Lluis.

The concierge was effusive. "I have a wonderful room for you," he said. "But if there is anything else we can do for you, you must let me know."

He handed me a room key and waved at the porter. I said my good-byes to Lluis and then followed the porter to the eleva-tors. My room was on the eighth floor. I took a deep breath when the doors opened and walked in quickly before I changed my mind.

When we arrived upstairs, the porter opened the door, settled my bags and then left. It was an elegant room: large and airy, with big windows that looked over the street and a park in the distance. An enormous vase of white tulips sat on a table by the window, and a basket of fruit and chocolate was on the dresser. I kicked off my shoes, flopped onto the king-sized bed and pulled out my phone.

When I had received Tessa's message, I'd written back immediately. Not to Tessa but to Nawang. What was she telling everyone? *Of course I'm coming back,* I wrote. *I don't always have good cell phone reception, but I am checking my inbox as often as I can. Please keep me informed of any problems or developments. I will do my best to respond as quickly as possible.*

During the flight from Mexico I had frequently returned to Tessa's message. It had snapped me out of my homesickness. First, it had made me worried again about my job. Was Nawang using my absence to maneuver herself into my position? I always felt I could trust her, but had I been naive? Or was this David's way of getting back at me for inconveniencing him? Was he suggesting to my clients that Nawang was now in charge?

While my mind was besieged with all sorts of paranoid thoughts, I could still hear the faint echo of Julian's words: *If we are mistrustful of others, we are distrustful of ourselves.* Perhaps I had to be on my toes, but this crazy worry would do no good at all. And I sure didn't like the way it was making me feel.

More discomfiting than my career concerns, however, was Tessa's personal message. Of course, there had been something between Tessa and me over the past few months. It was one of the things that perked me up when times were rough. After an argument with Annisha or a lonely night in the apartment, I would walk into the office and see Tessa's smiling face. But it was always an abstract kind of thing. Now, however, Tessa had made it concrete, real.

WHEN I ARRIVED BACK in the lobby at nine, I immediately spotted Lluis's dapper frame. He was standing next to one side of the doors, his hands behind his back, rocking back and forth slightly on his heels. He was obviously waiting for me, but the gentle smile on his face suggested that he didn't mind.

His cab was parked on the street outside the doors of the hotel. This time, he let me sit in the front seat with him. As we drove, Lluis chatted amiably.

"Too bad that you have so little time in this fantastic city," he said. "There is so much to see. I always say that this is a city of artistic brilliance."

We were clearly heading into a much older part of the city. The streets were becoming increasingly narrow and dark.

"Really?" I said.

"Oh, I know, when people think of exceptional artists they think of Florence, Rome, Paris. They think of the Uffizi or the Sistine Chapel or the Louvre. But Barcelona—Barcelona is the home of so many great artists of the last century. Joan Miró, Salvador Dalí, Pablo Picasso. And, of course, the brilliant architect Antoni Gaudí. Geniuses all."

I could sense that Lluis was on a roll. We were now in what must have been the Old City area; the patina of centuries clung to each building and cobbled alley. Some of the streets were so tight that I did not think the car would fit down them, but Lluis, talking all the while, his left hand gesturing in the air, maneuvered through them with ease. Our near-accident clearly hadn't rattled him.

"Yes, there are so many places in the world where you can see the magnificent works of Picasso. There are about fifty thousand of them after all. But where else in the world can you see the very beginnings of his specialness? Our Picasso museum has his earliest works—the sketches and paintings from his childhood in Spain. You can see the figure studies he did under his father's guidance. You can see what a brilliant eye he had, even then. It is really something to enjoy those early seeds of his later masterpieces."

We passed churches and a cathedral, low-rise buildings with ornate iron balconies above and arched doorways below. There were shops shuttered with corrugated steel doors, festooned with graffiti. But eventually we left the cramped streets and were again on major roadways. The ocean came into view. I could see yachts docked in the harbor, their lights twinkling on the black water. Palm trees lined the street, and the invigorating saltiness of the sea hung in the air.

"Barceloneta up ahead," Lluis said, as we moved past the port area. We turned up a side street away from the water. Lluis wove in and out of the tiny streets and eventually pulled into an alley. "We must walk from here," he said.

THE SMALL, INTIMATE RESTAURANT appeared to be full of locals. "Too far away from the water for tourists," said Lluis.

I looked at the menu. It was written in two languages, in

what Lluis explained was Spanish and Catalan. I could make out a few things, but not enough to figure out what I wanted. I looked up from the menu, and Lluis was smiling at me. "Do you like fish and shellfish?" he asked.

I nodded.

"Good," he said. "It is really a shame to eat in a Catalonian restaurant and not sample the fruits of the sea. Can I order for us?"

Our meal started with a smooth fish bisque, then a platter of grilled vegetables, followed by garlicky prawns, crispy squid and steamed grouper. Lluis ordered wine and filled my glass whenever it dipped low.

Before the food started to arrive, he reached into his pocket.

"I might as well give this to you now. I worry about losing it." Lluis handed me a brown leather box. It was about four inches long and two inches wide, with a hinged lid. I lifted the brass clasp and opened the top. Lying on top of a piece of folded parchment was a thin, delicate paintbrush. The handle was of smooth dark wood topped with a tuft of fine bristles. I picked up the paintbrush and twirled it gently between my thumb and forefinger. Then I placed it carefully on the table and pulled out the note.

The note was written in black ink. Its neat writing read:

*To Lead Your Best Life, Do Your Best Work*
*There is no insignificant work in the world. All labor is a chance to express personal talents, to create our art and to realize the genius we are built to be. We must work like Picasso painted: with devotion, passion, energy and excellence. In this way, our productivity will not only become a source of inspiration to others, but it will have an impact—making a difference in the lives around us. One of*

*the greatest secrets to a life beautifully lived is to do work that mat-
ters. And to ascend to such a state of mastery in it that people can't
take their eyes off of you.*

I put the paintbrush back in the box and slipped it into my
pocket. I would transfer the paintbrush to my pouch and the
note into my journal when I got back to my hotel room.

"An interesting sentiment, isn't it?" said Lluis.

"Yes," I said. "Picasso. Genius-level work. I suppose that is
why you are the safekeeper of this particular talisman. Your
interest in all of those creative masters, right?"

Lluis laughed.

"Perhaps," he said. "But I think there's more to it than that."

Lluis explained to me that he had met Julian years ago when,
by chance, Julian was one of his fares from the airport. Lluis
was then driving a cab to pay his way through college. Julian
was on a stopover, so he wasn't going to have much time in Barcelona. He had asked Lluis what he should do, what he should
see if he had only one day in the city. Lluis had so much to say,
so many ideas and and so much information to exchange that
they talked for a considerable time after they reached the hotel.
Eventually Julian asked Lluis if he would like to join him for
dinner.

"I brought Julian to this same restaurant," said Lluis. "And
we have stayed in touch since then. I think it is everything that
has happened to me since that first meeting that made Julian
think of me when he was looking for safekeepers for the talismans."

As we moved from course to course, Lluis told me his story.
He had spent his childhood in a tiny village south of Barce-

lona, along the Mediterranean coast. When he was fourteen, his family moved to the city.

"That was such an adventure for me. From a sleepy little village to this." Lluis swept his hand in front of him. "I know that it is not such a common thing for a young boy, but I loved the galleries. And the history. But most of all, I loved the streets. To be able to walk down La Rambla and see a Miró mosaic, right there, on the ground in front of you. Or to come across a Picasso sculpture, or some medieval church or bit of Roman wall as you wandered through the Barri Gòtic. I would take my bike and spend my spare time crisscrossing the city, to see what I could see."

When Lluis finished high school, there was much debate in the family about the direction he should take. His father, a businessman, wanted him to become a lawyer. His mother, whose family, like Chava's, had never attended university, didn't care as long as he went to school.

Eventually it was an aunt who suggested that he should channel his knowledge and love of the city into a college program in tourism and the hospitality industry.

"My father was disappointed. 'No ambition,' he said. He really wanted me to be an attorney, or at least some kind of professional. A neurosurgeon, maybe. Or an orthodontist."

"An electrical engineer?" I said.

"That would do. But a hotel manager? To my dad, that didn't quite cut it. Owning the hotel, yes. Working for it, no."

Lluis tried to ignore his dad. He enrolled, went to classes and drove a cab to pay for it all. When he was done, he got a position in the hotel I was now staying at. He worked as assistant desk manager. Then assistant concierge. Then head concierge.

"It wasn't long after that I moved into upper management. I was the youngest hotel manager in the city."

But then, at the end of a very long day, Lluis walked out of the hotel and saw an old friend from his taxi-driving days opening the door of his cab for a hotel guest. He smiled at Lluis and waved, then hopped in the cab and drove off. Lluis watched with a heavy heart as the tail-lights disappeared down the street. Lluis had got to work that morning before the sun was up. He was leaving just as the sun slipped down the horizon. He had barely left his office all day; he hadn't once stepped outside. It felt as if he had spent his work hours in some sort of suspended animation. And all the time, the world was spinning. Clouds were moving across the sky, birds were calling, people were moving back and forth through the city. The whole place was alive, while he had been without a pulse.

"I had never felt that way when I drove that cab. I always felt energetic, alive, a part of the world. At that moment, on that sidewalk, standing in my expensive suit and freshly polished shoes, I made a decision. I would resign from the hotel. I would go back to the only job I had ever really loved. I would drive a cab."

Lluis paused and took a sip of his wine.

"And you are happy? Was it the right decision?" I asked.

"Absolutely."

"Is your father still disappointed?" I asked.

"Oh yes," said Lluis. "We don't speak of it anymore, but he treats me as if I'm doing a stint in prison. And you know what the irony is, Jonathan? What really saddens me? This is a man who hates what he does. His own father forced him into the family business, made him take over when my grandfather retired. And every day that my father has run that business has been an agony to him. He swore he'd never make any of his children join the company. He's just counting the days till he can retire and sell the place."

Lluis was staring at the tabletop, shaking his head. Just then the waiter came by and put our desserts in front of us. When he left, I looked back at Lluis.

"Why doesn't your father walk away right now?" I asked.

"Well," said Lluis, "as you might imagine, because he hates it so much, he isn't very good at it. It's like a joke one of my customers told me: How do you make a small fortune in a bad economy?"

I shook my head.

"Start with a *large* one," said Lluis. We both laughed. Then Lluis's smile faded.

"The company isn't worth much anymore, but my father slogs along each day, hoping he can rebuild it and retire a wealthy man. But at this point, I have more chance of riches than he does."

We were quiet for a moment. Lluis picked a strawberry out of his fruit salad but then let it drop back into his bowl.

"So Julian gave you this talisman because you chose to do something you love?" I asked. It didn't seem like a perfect fit: is doing what you love necessarily the same thing as doing "your best work"?

"No, I don't think that's exactly why I was given this particular talisman," said Lluis. "I think Julian gave me this one because of a promise I made to myself that day on the sidewalk. I knew that my friends and family would question my decision. And I decided that I never wanted to feel apologetic about my work. I always wanted to feel proud of myself. And the only way to do that would be to do the very best job I could."

Lluis looked across at me and smiled.

"That young cabbie who almost hit us today—he doesn't understand how to drive well. He thinks that to get your passengers where they are going as quickly as possible you have to speed, take foolish chances. He doesn't realize that the fastest way to move between point A and point B is to know the city—to choose the best route and to avoid the problem areas. That's what I do. There isn't a street or alleyway I don't know. But being the best cabbie I can be is more than just driving efficiently. When I am taking visitors around Barcelona, I can answer any question they put to me—what restaurant serves the best *fideuà*, what are the hours of the Museum of Contemporary Art, where is the finest place to shop for antiques? And if a customer gets off a plane at twelve at night, craving an American-style hotdog, I know where to take him.

"Julian gave the talisman to me because I believe with all my heart that a job is just a job only if you see it as just a job. Some may say I'm 'just a taxi driver.' But to me, I help visitors create memories that enrich their lives. I have the chance to show people some decency in a world where so many among us long for more human connections. I get to put smiles on the faces of my customers—and leave them better than I found them. In my mind, work is a vehicle for discovering more of our gifts, displaying more of our potential and being of use to other human beings."

Our coffee had arrived now, and we both fell silent as we took our first sips. I don't know what Lluis was thinking about, but my thoughts were with my dad, back in the classroom so many years ago.

Before we parted for the night, Lluis offered to share more of his genius. He would pick me up in the morning and give me a tour of his city. We agreed to meet at eight o'clock.

WHEN THE ALARM went off at six a.m. the next morning, I almost rolled over and went back to sleep. But I thought of that word I had written in my journal: *push-ups*. I lumbered out of bed and staggered to my luggage. I had packed a set of workout clothes. Whenever I traveled for business I did this— the shorts, T-shirt, gym shoes and socks invariably remaining in their state of readiness until I unpacked them again back at home. But this morning, instead of lying in bed and thinking up reasons not to go to the hotel gym, I got up and pulled on the clothes before my body had the opportunity to object. I was more than my limitations, I was learning. And it seemed to me that all the excuses I used to make were nothing more than lies that my fears had been trying to sell me. I shuffled into the bathroom, brushed my teeth, splashed some cold water on my face and then grabbed my hotel key and headed out the door. It wasn't until twenty minutes later—jogging on the treadmill, my eyes firmly glued on a TV newscast I couldn't understand— that my brain woke up and I became fully aware of what I was doing. The first thing my functioning brain did was congratulate myself.

After my run, I did the push-ups I'd promised in the journal and a few sit-ups on the incline board. Then I headed back to my room to get ready.

After an indulgently long shower, I got dressed and headed to the lobby. The head concierge was not on duty yet, but the assistant concierge directed me to a café on the corner that was supposed to have the best coffee around.

While I ate my breakfast, I went through my messages. There was a conciliatory note from Nawang assuring me that she was keeping me in the loop and saying how much she was looking forward to my return. There were a host of other forwarded and cc-ed notes, making me wonder if Nawang had belatedly realized that she had dropped me from the correspondence thread. I responded to most, if only to let everyone know I was still kicking. And then I returned to Tessa's note.

I read it and reread it, but no amount of reviewing it was going to help. I just didn't know how to respond. Instead, I pulled out the journal Julian had given me. Maybe writing out my thoughts would help clarify things. The truth was that Tessa had been on my mind—a lot. But it was also true that the idea of encouraging her—the thought of starting a new relationship—terrified me and filled me with guilt. I was still married, after all. But how long would that last? Certainly in the months after Annisha had asked me to leave, I thought of the separation as only a temporary arrangement. I knew that Annisha was trying to force me to reconsider my priorities, but I had assumed the separation would force *her* to accept that what we had together was better than life apart. Now I wasn't so sure that Annisha would ever see that. Her frustration and anger had softened, but it seemed to be replaced with sadness and resignation—not regret. Did that mean she had moved on? Was it over?

And if it was, what could be so wrong about seeing Tessa? Maybe it was the workplace romance thing. No one ever *recommends* that. Or was it just the fear of something new, of change or the unknown? What had Julian said in that note he wrote about the grinning-skull talisman—embrace your fears? Maybe that was what I should do here—face the nerve-racking agony of asking someone out. After all, it had worked for me before. I closed the journal and put my pen back in my pocket, suddenly lost in an onslaught of memory.

I first noticed Annisha in my elective ancient history course. I had taken it because it was the only half-credit course I could find that fit into my engineering schedule. It was not an uninteresting class, but what kept me coming to the lectures was the girl who sat near the front of the room, on the right side. I tried to sit as close to her as possible while still far enough away that I could get a good look at her profile if she turned her head. She had almond-shaped eyes and long, glossy-black hair. And even when she wasn't smiling, her face had a cheerful expression. She didn't say much in class, but when she did, she was always worth listening to. I spent the whole year wondering how I might strike up a conversation with her, with no success. By the time the final exam rolled around, I realized I had blown my chance. Since she was in arts and I was in engineering, the odds that we would have another class together again, or even cross paths, were negligible. I spent my summer in an orgy of recrimination and self-loathing.

Third year unfolded with no Annisha sightings. I had a couple of unsuccessful relationships and another lonely summer. Then, in my senior year, the gods smiled on me.

During the first week back at school, my roommates and I headed to the campus bar on Friday night. It was something

of a ritual—checking out the new waitresses. To our disappointment, we ended up at a table with a male server. There
were a few familiar faces among the wait staff, a few new girls,
but it wasn't until I headed for the bathroom that I noticed
the woman serving in the back corner. It was Annisha. When
I got back to my table, I leaned over to Evan and asked him to
look at the girl serving near the bar. He raised himself from his
seat and peered across the room just as Annisha turned in our
direction.

"Hmm," he said, "what . . . do . . . I . . . think?" He settled
back into his chair. "What I think is . . . she's *waaay* out of your
league."

It wasn't the response I was looking for. I was hoping he might
say something so glowing that I would be propelled past my fear,
or something that made it clear that I would have to move before
he did. But he slumped in front of his beer and smirked at me.
"Honestly, Jonathan. Forget it," he said unhelpfully.

I spent the evening nursing my beer and summoning my
courage. As my roommates stood to leave, I told them that I
had to go to the bathroom and they should head home without
me. Evan looked over at me and raised an eyebrow.

"Yeah, good luck with that," he said as he hauled on his jacket.
His tone suggested luck had little to do with it—I needed nothing less than divine intervention.

I could see Annisha sitting at a table near the bar. Her sec-
tion was empty. She appeared to be counting her tips. I walked
over and hovered near the table, but she didn't seem to notice
I was there.

"Hi," I said eventually.

"Oh, hi." She smiled when she looked up, and kept smiling

when she saw it was me. Either she was very nice or it was a good sign. Maybe both.

"Sorry to bug you," I said. "Umm. I think you were in my ancient history class in second year?"

Annisha tilted her head to one side and paused, as if in thought. After a moment she said, "The engineer, right?" She said it slowly, as if she was still searching her memory as she spoke.

"Right, right," I said. "It was my elective."

I realized that I had started to shift my weight from foot to foot. I forced myself to stand still. Then I blurted it out.

"I was just wondering if you wanted to go out for coffee sometime?"

She was still smiling, but she didn't respond right away. She was clearly weighing the idea.

"This is kind of a busy week," she said. "I'm catching up with a lot of friends I haven't seen since last year."

I started nodding my head, composing my response, trying to think of something to say that would make it sound as if I really didn't care that she didn't want to see me.

"But next week I should have time." She was ripping a small piece of paper from the receipts piled in front of her. She wrote a phone number on it and handed it to me.

"My name is Annisha, by the way," she said. "I'm sorry. I've forgotten yours."

LLUIS SHOWED UP in front of the hotel right at eight a.m. He wasn't in his taxi.

"I thought we could start by walking," he said. "I love to drive, but walking is the best way to see the city."

Lluis had convinced me the previous night that I should spend what little time I had in Barcelona looking at the architecture. He claimed it was one of Barcelona's major contributions to the world of art.

"We have nine buildings that are UNESCO heritage sites. And there is Gaudí and all that wonderful Catalan modernism architecture you saw yesterday afternoon. But architecture isn't some artifact of the past in Barcelona. We care deeply about our buildings still today."

Lluis explained that the city was home to more than five thousand working architects. "I challenge you to find more architects per capita anywhere else in the world," he said. I didn't take him up on that. He told me about buildings by Jean Nouvel, Zaha Hadid, Frank Gehry, Richard Rogers. Gehry's was the only name I recognized, but I didn't like to admit that.

With just a short break for an early lunch, we spent the morning and afternoon walking and walking. Occasionally we hopped on a bus, but most of the time we strolled along, our necks craned up, our heads moving back and forth to take in the buildings around us.

We saw Gaudí's La Pedrera apartments. With their wavy walls, look of water-worn stone, and seaweedy iron balconies, it made me think of the lost city of Atlantis. Surely a city at the bottom of the ocean would look like this. We wandered through Parc Güell with the mushroom-topped gatehouse, the mosaic lizard sculpture, the circular tile-adorned esplanade. And we ended our day back where we had been last evening, in front of Sagrada Família, Gaudí's unfinished testament to his vision and his faith, according to Lluis.

"I love this place," said Lluis thoughtfully, gazing up at the four soaring spires. "Did I tell you that my great-grandfather worked on it?"

"Really?" I said. "Was he a stone mason?"

"No," said Lluis. "Just a laborer, I believe. I suspect he spent a lot of time pushing wheelbarrows and hauling bricks. But you know, like Julian's note says, there is no insignificant work. I like to think of him sweating and dirty, looking up at the end of a long day, seeing this magnificent church rising above him and knowing that without his muscle and his time, something like this would simply not happen."


IT WAS LATE AFTERNOON when Lluis walked me back to the hotel. He had some errands to run, and we both wanted to make it an early evening. My flight left at eight the next morning, and Lluis insisted on picking me up at five to get me there.

Once in my suite, I ordered dinner from room service. I wrote a couple of notes in my journal, and then pulled out my phone and composed a short message to Adam. The longing I had felt for him in Mexico lingered. I wondered how I could have gone so many days without phoning or visiting him when I was home. I started the note with a plaintive "I miss you so much, buddy." But then I thought of Adam's sad eyes when I had kissed him good-bye before flying to Istanbul. I erased the sentence. I wanted to be there for him, even if only with a note, rather than underlining my absence. Instead I wrote about the Temple of the Magician and about the Mayan ruins I had seen. I wrote about the sounds of the birds in the trees and the pumas that roam the forests of the Yucatán—and how I was mighty glad I didn't meet any. And then I told him I had just spent the day in Barcelona. *Remember last summer when we made castles on the beach and we dribbled wet sand to make the tops tall and pointy? That's what the church I saw yesterday looked like. It was covered with spiky towers. It was designed by a guy named Antoni Gaudí, and I bet that when he was a boy, he made sand castles just like you.*

I paused for a second, thinking about my next sentence. Then I wrote, *When I get back, I will take you to the beach for a weekend.* I knew the dangers of making promises, but I was determined to keep this one. It would break my heart, as well as Adam's, if I didn't.

THE EARLY MORNING LIGHT was still breaking across the horizon when Lluis let me out of the taxi at the terminal the next day. He was bright and cheerful as usual, but he obviously noticed that I was still engulfed in my early morning fog. As he pulled my suitcase from the trunk, he looked at me with concern. "Are you sure you have everything, Jonathan?" he said. I patted my pocket to check for my wallet and passport, and then I had a momentary rush of panic. The talismans. Was the pouch around my neck? I couldn't feel it. I opened my jacket and patted my shirt front, and sure enough, there it was—a lumpy little bag lying next to my skin. How could I have missed it? I was surprised that while it was heavier than it ever had been, the leather string did not seem to be cutting into my neck anymore. I took the pouch out from under my shirt and shoved it in my pocket. I would have to stick it in one of the plastic tubs at security.

ONCE I HAD CHECKED IN and reached the departures lounge, I found a quiet corner and dialed Annisha. It would be late—midnight, I guessed—but I was longing to talk with her, to hear some news of Adam.

When Annisha answered the phone, I apologized about the hour, but she sounded relieved to hear from me. "I'm so glad you called," she said. "There was a little incident at school today that I wanted to talk about with you. Apparently—"

Annisha stopped. I could hear a tiny voice in the background.

"Mommy," Adam was saying, "I can't sleep."

"Oh dear," I could hear Annisha reply. "Come here and sit with Mommy. Do you want to talk to Daddy about what's keeping you up?"

When Adam got on the phone, I asked him how he was.

"Fine," he said in a quiet voice.

"What's new?" I tried again.

"Nothing," he said. Then I heard Annisha in the background.

"You wanted to tell Daddy what happened at school today, remember?"

With a little coaxing on my part, and a little prompting on Annisha's, Adam told me that one of the second-grade students had tripped him, pushed him down and taken his granola bar at lunch.

"What did you do?" I asked. Adam said he'd told his teacher, Ms. Vanderwees, who was on yard duty. Ms. Vanderwees sent the older boy to the office.

"Did that ever happen to you?" asked Adam. "When you were little, were other kids ever bullies?"

I told Adam all about Phil Stefak, who stole all my baseball cards and teased me about my glasses. I told him how Phil used to follow me home from school and shout strings of insults. I explained that I had been afraid to tell anyone, but finally when Phil actually grabbed my glasses from my face and stepped on them, I told my teacher. I never really found out what happened. But after that, Phil only glared at me. He never touched me again. We talked for a long time before Annisha took the phone back from Adam. I looked at my watch.

"Sorry," I said to Annisha. "You must both be exhausted."

"That's okay," said Annisha. "He really needed to talk to you. But I should try to get him back to sleep now."

"Sure," I said. "Just one more thing—do you know what the school is doing about this kid?"

Annisha told Adam to head back to his room, and she would join him there in a minute. Then she told me that Ms. Vanderwees had phoned her after lunch. This wasn't the first time the boy had bullied other students. The principal called his parents and asked them to come in for a talk. Ms. Vanderwees also said she would go out for yard duty as much as she could in the coming week so she could keep an eye on things. And she had talked to the whole class about being helpful bystanders when they saw another child being hurt in the school yard.

"She is taking it really seriously," said Annisha. "I felt a lot better after I talked with her."

Annisha and I chatted a little bit more about Adam and school and then I said goodnight.

THE DEPARTURE LOUNGE was quite crowded now. Most of the seats were full. Men and women with briefcases and laptops. A few parents with small children. And across from me, a teenage girl, earphones on her head, slumped in her seat, glaring at her mother who was offering her a piece of gum.

I thought of my surly teenage self. My parents' patience with me. I felt a familiar ache beneath my ribs. I missed my father.

Sitting there in the Barcelona airport, thinking about my son being watched over by Ms. Vanderwees, remembering my dad and my own childhood, it struck me that my five-year-old self had got it right. My dad was a classroom genius, working in a truly noble profession. He had achieved the greatness Lluis aspired to. I had a lot of work to do if I wanted to come close to being the man he became.

# Chapter Eight

WHILE I WAS IN SPAIN, Julian had sent me some information about my next two destinations. The first one would land me back in North America, sending me to Cape Breton Island, on the east coast of Canada.

So, with a connection in London and one in Halifax, and more than sixteen hours after Lluis had left me at the airport in Barcelona, I landed in Sydney, in Cape Breton, Nova Scotia. It was early evening. As Julian had promised, a rental car was waiting for me. I was relieved to find it had a GPS. I realized that I had no real idea about how to get from Sydney to St. Ann's.

"It'll take you about an hour," said the fellow at the rental agency.

The safekeeper here was a woman named Mary McNeil. I sent her a message to tell her I was on my way.

As I pulled out of Sydney and hit the highway, I was reminded of what I had seen of the Yucatán Peninsula. Not the weather, or the houses, or the vegetation. No, here the air was crisp and cool; the firs and balsams and birches, thick and deep green. And water. There was water everywhere. The road twisted and turned—I could see from the GPS that my route was almost circuitous, but after every few miles of trees and woods, an expanse of water—some bay or lake—would flicker into view. What reminded me of the Yucatán was the sparseness of the population on Cape Breton. Like leaving Mérida, as soon as I exited Sydney I felt as if I had left people behind. I drove past vast stretches where hardly anyone lived. A house or two might pop up on the roadside only to slide into the rearview mirror, vanishing into a sea of trees. There was something, however, about traveling through this remote place to meet someone, even if that someone was a stranger, that was comforting. At the end of this journey, I thought, a person is waiting for me.

Mary McNeil and Angus Macdonald lived just off a scenic highway called the Cabot Trail, across the road from St. Ann's Bay. In a message, Mary had said I would see a mailbox at the side of the road, and a post with a number, but I wouldn't be able to see the house until I'd driven some distance down the lane. Luckily, the GPS did the work for me, and before long I was climbing up a gravel road, thick bush on either side, the pitch of a roof peeking above the trees ahead of me. She must have been looking out the window because as soon I pulled the car behind the two trucks at the side of the house, a tall woman with salt-and-pepper hair was on the front steps waving at me. That had to be Mary, I thought.

By the time I had stepped out of the car, Mary was by my side, as was a man who I assumed was her husband, Angus. He was slightly shorter than Mary, definitely rounder, and with a warm smile that matched her own. Neither grabbed me like Lluis had, but Angus patted me on the shoulder and Mary held my hand in both of hers as she introduced herself. They seemed happy to see me, but Mary's eyes were pinched, as if with concern. "You must be so tired," she said. "Angus, Angus," she continued with some alarm, gesturing at the backseat of the car. In the next moment, Angus and I were wrestling over my baggage in what must have looked like a cartoon dust-up. I finally relented and let him carry everything into the house for me.

"I understand from Julian that you've been on quite a journey," Mary said. "So we've got a little supper ready for you, and then you can disappear to bed if you'd like. I imagine it's almost midnight Spain time."

Mary and Angus led me into the living room. It was eclectically furnished, and there were a couple of enormous canvases on the wall. One looked like a vaguely aquatic scene—brilliant turquoise and green with dark shadows dancing across the color. The other was a pastiche of colored blocks that seemed to rearrange themselves before my eyes. Mary pointed me to a deep chair that faced a bank of windows. When I sat down, I immediately noticed the most spectacular thing in the room. A great wave of green swept before me and at its end a thin strip of dark blue—St. Ann's Bay, and the waters of the Atlantic Ocean.

"Sit, sit," said Angus. "I'll just get things on the table and then call you both."

Mary brought me a beer and then sat down next to me. She asked a few questions about my travels.

"It sounds as if you've been very busy. You may just want to rest tomorrow, but Angus and I were thinking of doing a few things with you."

I was not surprised. Antoine in Paris was, so far, the only safekeeper who left me to my own devices. I had mixed feelings. After sitting on so many long flights, it was probably good to be busy. But I wasn't sure if I felt like a lot of planned activity.

Mary said that if I was up to it, she was hoping to have a small dinner party in my honor the next night.

"Nothing fancy," she assured me. "Just a few friends and relatives. And lobsters. It's lobster season, so I thought you might enjoy that."

I smiled and said that sounded delightful, but in my heart, I wasn't so sure. Mary also said she was planning to spend the day getting ready for the party, while Angus drove me around the Cabot Trail—a loop of roadway that circled the mountains of the Cape Breton Highlands on the northern end of the island.

"It's beautiful," Mary said. "I've lived here almost my whole life, and I never tire of it."

I said I hadn't done that before and would love to see this part of the world. "I've heard it reminds people of the green hills of Ireland," I said.

Mary nodded. "Yes, but somehow wilder. At least that's how it strikes me."

I had been traveling now for about two weeks, but in truth I had lost any real sense of time. I was tired and homesick, but my anxiety about work and all the urgency I felt about getting back to it were becoming strangely muted. I knew I should be worried, but it was as if I no longer had the energy. I might have insisted that I fly back out the next day, I might have tried to hurry the trip along, but I no longer wanted to do that. A long drive might be just the thing.

It was only a few minutes later when Angus's voice came from the kitchen.

"Time to chow down," he called out. Mary picked up my glass and led the way.

The kitchen was huge, but not fancy. A pine harvest table stretched out on one side of the room—circled by eight high-back chairs. An old-fashioned sideboard was crammed with bits of antique china and bright, hand-blown glass bowls. There were some colorful prints on the walls around the table.

Angus placed a steaming pan of lasagna on a trivet in the center of the table. There was already a green salad there, and a basket of bread.

"I don't know how hungry you are, Jonathan, so I'll just let you help yourself," he said.

I was not in the mood to talk about myself, and I knew the best way to deflect any demand for that was by asking the questions. Angus, I learned, was a dentist with a practice in Baddeck. He had grown up in Glace Bay, the son of a coal miner. In fact, all the men in his family had worked the mines, until his dad's youngest brother headed out to Moncton in New Brunswick, where he eventually became an accountant. Angus had met Mary when the two of them were in university, but they hadn't dated until they were in their thirties. Mary was an artist and worked in a studio up the hill, behind the house.

"It has the most beautiful light," said Mary.

I asked them how they came to know Julian. Mary told me she had met him many, many years ago, when she was a young artist working in New York City.

"Julian bought a number of my pieces," she said. "This was when he was a litigation lawyer and was spending money like a drunken sailor." Mary laughed at that. "We lost touch for a while, and then after I'd moved back here, he found me."

"He must have been a big fan of your work to track you here," I said.

"No," said Mary. "This was after he had returned from Sivana. He got in touch with me just to talk."

I thought about my old high school friends, my college roommates, all the people I had inadvertently lost touch with over the years. And then there were the people I had deliberately ignored. I felt a twinge in my chest. Juan fell into that second category. After my lunch with David and Sven, Juan had come to see me a few times. He was confused. David and Sven had accosted him with an avalanche of demands. Set up nearly impossible goals with completely unrealistic deadlines. They asked for reports and accounting so frequently that it was almost a joke. Except Juan was not laughing. He became worried, anxious and stressed. Each time he talked with me, I claimed complete ignorance. When he asked me to intervene, to act as an unofficial liaison between the design department and upper management, I waffled. Eventually I began to avoid him.

Juan was not a stupid man. He could see that I had no desire to get involved. He stopped coming by my office. But I would see him in the hallways, looking troubled and gaunt, deep lines carved down his face, his eyes pouchy and sad. One of the last times I spoke with him, he had caught me by surprise in the company parking lot.

"Ah, Jonathan, I know you know what's going on," he said sadly. "And I know there is nothing anyone can do to help. But

I'm a fifty-five-year-old man. I can't afford to retire yet, but if I quit. . . Well, who is going to hire an old guy like me?" Then he climbed into his car and pulled out of the lot.

It was only a month later when the news buzzed through the office. Juan's car had flown off the road the previous evening on his way home from work. He was dead by the time the ambulance arrived.

THE LASAGNA WAS DELICIOUS, but the combination of the rich food and the time difference was making my eyes heavy. Angus cleared the dishes from the table, but Mary stayed sitting.

"I know you need to get to bed now," she said. "But I'd like to give you the talisman tonight. Actually, I was going to give it to you tomorrow just before the party. I decided to have the party because of the talisman. I thought it would be appropriate— the right kind of way to celebrate the hand-off. But I know me. I'll be flying in all directions at once tomorrow, getting dinner ready, so now might be a better time."

Mary took a small padded envelope from her pocket and put it in the center of the table. But she kept her hand over it.

"Before you open this," said Mary, "may I see the other talismans?"

I was so used to the feel of the soft suede on my skin, the gentle weight against my chest. I was surprised by how reluctant I was to lose the comfort of the pouch, to take it off. But I drew it out from under my shirt and lifted it from my neck. I opened the top and very gently slid the talismans onto the table.

Mary looked carefully at the small assortment.

"Julian must think very highly of you, must care about you deeply, to entrust you with this task," she said.

"Well, I don't know," I said. "He and my mother are close. But I don't really know him."

"But he clearly knows *you*," said Mary. She was smiling softly.

She reached toward the center of the table and picked up the grinning skull.

"Embrace your fears," she said. I nodded.

She put the skull down and reached for the crane.

"Kindness." She placed the crane in front of her, next to the skull.

"Small daily improvements." She was running her fingers over the little pyramid.

She put the red clay piece on the table and picked up the paintbrush. Like I had done when I first got it, she twirled the dark wood between her fingers.

"All work can be a means of creative self-expression," she said.

"How do you know all this?" I asked her.

Mary looked up at me and tilted her head, as if trying to decide something.

"These talismans," she eventually said, waving her hand over the small pile on the table, "there is only one of each of these things. But they are symbols, after all. Julian has talked about their wisdom for years. And I've been listening."

Finally, Mary picked up the sun and moon amulet.

"Ah," she said. "Live your authentic life. This is a very good one. This one is so important, but few people make use of this truth."

She put the piece down on the table, and looked at me.

"Can I ask you something, Jonathan? Something personal?" I didn't really feel I could say no.

"Do you think you are being true to yourself? Do you think you are leading the life you are meant to live—the one that most honors the real you, celebrates your deepest values and respects your highest dreams?"

I blanched, lifted my tea mug to my mouth to stall a little. Mary was looking at me intently. I couldn't fathom why she would be so interested in me or the answer to that question. I took a sip of tea, and then put my cup back down.

"I . . . I don't know," I stammered. "I've been trying to figure that out during this trip."

"I understand," said Mary. "It's a tough one."

"I mean, I think maybe I'm not," I offered. "But I'm just not sure what my authentic life would look like. I am beginning to rethink my work, but I'm not sure about the rest of it."

Mary nodded.

"Since I've been prying into your life, maybe I should tell you a bit more about mine."

"Sure," I said. Anything not to have to talk more about myself.

Mary had told me earlier that she was a painter, but she said that her story wasn't one about rebellion. She hadn't become an artist because her family had wanted her to become an accountant. Nor had she had an epiphany one day while working at a nine-to-five job that her real passion was art. She had always known she wanted to be an artist, even as a child. It's what made her happy. Drawing, painting, sculpting, making things, it's all she ever wanted to do.

"Like Picasso," I said. I was remembering what Lluis had told me about his childhood. But Picasso's father was an artist, too. He encouraged the young Picasso. I asked Mary if her parents were artists.

"Good grief no. My dad had a fishing boat; my mom worked part-time at a grocery store," Mary said. "But they are amazing people, and they thought it was a great gift that I had something I loved so much. They just wanted me to keep doing it."

"And they weren't concerned about how you would make a living?" I asked.

Mary laughed. "My dad used to always say, 'Well, you'd be hard-pressed to make less money than your mother or me— but go ahead and try!'"

Her family was never affluent, but they were joyful. The prospect of being a starving artist didn't scare Mary. She won a scholarship to study fine arts in university in Halifax. Then she graduated and moved to Manhattan. She waited tables, and she painted. She worked her way into the art scene there. She started to exhibit. Eventually she was able to quit waitressing and paint full-time. She worked hard at making her living by painting and printmaking, but she was lucky, too.

"Right place, right time, I guess," Mary said.

"So you were living your authentic life, being true to yourself and all of that," I said.

Mary looked into her mug for a few seconds before she spoke. "Well, that's the interesting thing. I really thought I was, all those years in Manhattan. I was young, successful. I had friends, an active social life. It was exciting."

"So what wasn't real about it? What was wrong?" I said. Now she had me curious.

"What a lot of people don't realize is that the art scene can be pretty competitive. You know, who gets into what galleries, who gets attention from the critics, who's got the buzz and who doesn't. There can be a lot of shuffling for position, a lot of infighting and backbiting."

I must have looked surprised because Mary nodded her head and said, "Really."

Mary explained that another young artist, whose style and approach was similar to hers, arrived in Manhattan from Los Angeles. Suddenly he was at every gallery opening, every party, every artistic event. And wherever he was, he would make a beeline to Henri, the man who ran the galleries that were displaying and selling Mary's work. Mary knew Henri wouldn't take on the new artist while he represented her because his style was too similar to Mary's. But that didn't mean he might not drop Mary and take on the fresh face.

"That just sent me into a tailspin," Mary said.

Henri had made it possible for her to stop waiting on tables. And with his help, she had become the darling of the art critics for a while. But she could easily slip back into obscurity. Mary realized then that while she owed Henri a great deal, she didn't trust him. He was a canny businessman, never bogged down by loyalty or guilt. She could see she was slipping from his favor. And she could see that Henri wasn't the only one who thought Mary's star was fading. Some of Mary's friends stopped calling so often. There were dinner parties that she was not invited to. She dropped off the A-list for some gallery openings. One night at a film premiere, Mary found herself sharing a piece of gossip she'd heard about the Los Angeles painter with a writer for a local arts magazine.

"It was something about his time in California, something that reflected badly on his artistic integrity. I told the writer because I thought it might make him look like a flash in the pan. A poseur who wasn't going to be in the art world for long. I thought it would make me look like a more serious talent by comparison."

Mary went home that night disgusted with herself. She had never bad-mouthed anyone, and her behavior made her feel small, petty, desperate.

"I kept asking myself why I had done it. What had got me to that place," Mary said. "And that led me to take a long, hard look at the people in my life."

She realized that the people fell into two categories, more or less. The people whom she trusted and loved, who were true friends, who made her feel secure and happy, who always brought out the best in her. And then there was another group. People who might interest or entertain her—who she might be attracted to for all sorts of reasons but were also negative in some way. Some of them were funny but mean-spirited. (I thought of my old roommate Evan, and his "good luck with that.") Some of them interesting but angry. Some clearly saw everything as a competition—and because they were always comparing themselves with her, she compared herself with them. And then there were some who, through no fault of their own, really, just had an overall bad effect on her. Whenever she went out with one woman she always drank too much. Another guy was such a pessimist that she felt dispirited for days after she talked with him. Another was so laid-back that she would find herself sleeping in until noon if she spent too much time with him.

"You know," Mary said a little sadly, "Julian was part of that second group back then."

Mary decided that she needed to spend more time with the first group and less with the latter. But then she realized something else. There were a lot of people missing from both lists.

"My family was so important to me, but I hardly ever got to see them."

She knew that when she was with her mother and father, her brothers and sisters, her aunts and uncles, she felt most herself. They brought out the best in her.

"I realized that my authentic life was in art, but it was also with my family. Living life in a way that is right for you is sometimes about finding all the different elements you need."

Mary decided to go back to Cape Breton but not to Mabou, the small town where her parents lived. Instead she settled outside Baddeck, in St. Ann's, because at a SoHo art show she had met and befriended Christine, a wonderful sculptor who lived there. Tbe town was home to the Gaelic College of Celtic Arts and Crafts, and Christine had told her that the small community featured a number of accomplished artists and artisans.

"I knew it was also important for me to be surrounded by people who shared my passion, and who would inspire my own creativity, maybe push me a little. And that is why Julian asked me to take care of this particular talisman."

Mary pushed the padded envelope toward me. I tore open the top and pulled out a leaf of paper. With it came a small piece of carved wood. It was only an inch wide and half an inch high. And it was two hands, holding on to each other.

I unfolded the creamy parchment.

*Choose Your Influences Well*

*We do not move through our days alone or apart from the world around us. And so we must always be aware of the things and the people we allow into our lives. It's a mark of wisdom to choose to spend time in those places that inspire and energize you and associate with those people who elevate and uplift you. Whether in our work or within our personal lives, these most positive friends and peers will inspire us to be our greatest selves and to lead our largest lives.*

I folded the paper and slipped it into my pocket.

"I suppose tomorrow night I'm going to meet some of the positive people in your life," I said.

"Exactly," said Mary. She was slipping the talismans gently into the pouch. "Julian is one of them now. I just wish he could be here."

It was only ten o'clock, but it was three in the morning Barcelona time. Mary handed me the pouch and then showed me to a bedroom on the second floor.

"The bathroom is just down the hall, and I've put towels at the foot of your bed," she said. "Sleep well, and I'll see you tomorrow."

WHEN I WOKE UP the next morning, I felt as if I were crawling back to the world. I lay in bed for several minutes trying to figure out where I was. The smell of coffee and cinnamon wafted through the bedroom door. That's when I remembered—Cape Breton.

When I got into the kitchen, Angus and Mary were both

busy at the counters. "Please help yourself to coffee," said Mary. "The pancakes are almost ready—buttermilk apple."

There were blue pottery mugs beside the coffeepot. I took one and filled it up. The coffee was rich and strong and just what I needed. That's one of the things I had missed at the hotel in Barcelona and the inn in Kyoto. The warm aroma of breakfast drifting through a house.

Just as Mary placed a heaping platter of pancakes in the middle of the table, the phone rang. Angus picked it up, and almost immediately his brow creased.

"How many? Okay. Any other injuries? You're sure? All right, then. Keep the ice pack on his mouth, and I'll meet you at the office in half an hour."

Angus put the phone down and looked over at Mary. "Connor Ashton. Fell off his bike and broke his front teeth."

Then Angus turned to me. "I'm so sorry, Jonathan. It's an emergency—I have to rush."

I told him I understood completely, but my words trailed him as he disappeared out the door.

As Mary and I listened to his truck send gravel flying, Mary lifted some pancakes onto my plate.

"Oh dear," she sighed. "Now I don't know what to do. I should take you out, but I'm not sure how to do that and get ready for the dinner."

It occurred to me that this turn of events, as unfortunate as it was for little Connor Ashton, might just work quite nicely for me. I had a rental car; I could do the drive around the Cabot Trail on my own while Mary did what she had to do. Mary nodded at my suggestion.

"As long as you aren't afraid of heights, and you like driving, you'll be fine," said Mary. "You can't really get lost. It's a circle route and only about two hundred miles long. Just stay on the main road, and eventually you'll end up back here. But you'll want to stop often—at the lookouts and in some of the towns along the way."

After breakfast, Mary found a road map, and we sat down together. She circled places on the map, and on a separate piece of paper wrote down names of spots to visit and things to see. It turned into a very long list.

"Oh, I know, you can't do all this in one day. Pick and choose. And call me if you have any questions." Mary was filling a water bottle for me and putting some fruit and a sandwich in a bag. I told her not to worry about a lunch. I would stop in somewhere.

"Well," she said, "once you get into the highlands, you can drive for quite a while without finding any place to get food. You don't have to eat this, but it's there if you need it."


It was still early morning as my car carved through the Margaree Valley. Mary had suggested that I follow the Cabot Trail clockwise so that I would be on the inside lane when I started driving up and down the outside of the mountains. Right now, I was being enveloped by deep green hills on either side of me. I had driven for twenty minutes and had seen only a couple of cars. A hawk swooped down across the road, and out of the corner of my eye, I caught an occasional movement in the trees. Probably just a squirrel or a bird, but I wondered if I might come across a fox or a deer.

I started to think about Julian's note about influences and

people. And about Mary's decision about those she wanted to keep in her life. Her stories had made me think about friendships I would like to renew. And I would like to see more of my sister, Kira, and my mom. Kira especially always brought out the best in me. It was as if, in her presence, I remembered how to be someone a younger sister might look up to. And my mother—I took her for granted, I knew that. Her habit of telling me to put on a sweater or to finish my peas—even once I was grown and a father myself—sometimes had me racing out the door after Sunday dinner as if I were escaping a torture cell. But I also saw what a blessing it was to have been raised in her home. I was beginning to feel grateful for that. When I came through the door after a baseball game, she always asked, "Did you have fun?" instead of "Did you win?" And she managed to find something good to say about everybody—including Uncle Teddy, which was a feat of creativity to rival anything Picasso had pulled off. And when my father died, she showed a strength and bravery I couldn't have imagined in her before. Even in the early days after his passing, she showed more concern about the loss Kira and I had suffered than about her own. Her influence was certainly one I should return to, I thought.

But were there people who were dragging me down? People who were not positive elements in some way? David and Sven immediately sprang to mind, but I couldn't think of anyone in my personal life. Even when Annisha and I were fighting . . . I might not have behaved well, but was that her influence? Or was I just doing my best to win an argument? Annisha is one of the most optimistic people I know—which is probably why she stuck it out so long while I resisted her wishes at every turn. What about Tessa? She was lively and funny and beautiful. She actually reminded me of Annisha in many ways. I would like to keep her in my life, but in what fashion? I decided that when I next stopped the car, I would belatedly reply to her message. I would tell her the truth: I was in a state of transition; I was trying to figure out my life on many fronts. I appreciated her note, her thoughts, but I would have to talk to her about her proposal when I got back. I needed some time to sort myself out.

IT WAS BEFORE NOON when I entered Cape Breton Highlands National Park. For the next sixty miles the road would wind its way through the edge of the park as it circled the coast. Mary had suggested a short hike I might take at this end of the park. I was looking forward to getting out of the car, stretching my legs and eating my lunch.

I followed the signs for Le Chemin du Buttereau and eventually pulled into a small gravel parking lot. The sign at the foot of the trail said that the walk would take about ninety minutes. I looked around. It was a warm spring day, the sun high in an almost cloudless sky, but the parking lot was empty and there were no signs of anyone else about. Mary had warned me to be careful of coyotes. They usually didn't come near people, but there had been a recent attack on a hiker. I decided that I would eat my lunch in the car after my hike. Mary had given me a heavy walking stick, just to be on the safe side. I brought only it and the water bottle with me.

The dirt path was narrow and twisted, and it started to climb almost immediately. At some points, as I stepped up to the next tree root or boulder, I felt like I was mounting shallow stairs. The pine trees on either side of me were dense and left the spicy scent of sap lingering in the damp air. Birds called all around me, but other than that, the woods were silent.

Mary had told me that I would climb about two hundred feet over the course of a mile and a quarter before hitting a loop that ran around the top of the hill. "The view is spectacular from there," she said.

What she didn't tell me was that I would come across history as well. About twenty minutes into my climb, a sign appeared at the side of the trail. It announced that on my left I would see the remains of one of the last five homes of Le Buttereau—a French-Canadian farming settlement. I peered down the side of the hill, and sure enough, there among the trees and thick vegetation was a rough stone square—the foundations of a tiny house.

I knew I was in French-Canadian territory—Mary had also suggested I stop in the small Acadian fishing village of Chéticamp before I entered the park to see it firsthand.

So an hour before I started this hike, I had pulled off the highway and parked my car next to a restaurant on the water side of the road. A few shops and other buildings were wedged within the narrow strip of land between the road and Chéticamp Bay. Mary thought I might want to check out the hooked rugs, which were an area specialty, or to sample some *tchaude,* the local fish stew, but I didn't feel like being indoors. And I wasn't hungry enough to want to stop for a meal. Instead, I walked down the wooden stairs that ran between the shops and followed a boardwalk to a series of small docks. Modest commercial fishing boats, not unlike the one that Ahmet owned, lined the jetty. One dock had a large sign announcing whale-watching cruises. Another small fishing vessel was secured below the sign, near a Zodiac boat. Mary had suggested I might take a whale-watching tour in one of the old boats—the Zodiacs made noise and vibrations that disturbed the marine life. But I had decided that I would spend my time later on a hike instead.

Before I returned to my car, I walked back along the highway, until the restaurants and stores gave way to a line of modest wood-frame houses. A small stretch of sidewalk ran in front of them as the highway traffic sped by on the other side—almost on their doorsteps. Behind them I could see a narrow ribbon of green grass and then the water of the Gulf of St. Lawrence.

The Cabot Trail had once been a dirt road. It would have been a good deal narrower than it now was, and these homes would have perched precariously at its edge, the icy salt water lapping at their back doors. Mary had said that Chéticamp and the surrounding area was still French-speaking. The people were descendants of the Acadians who, in the mid-1700s, had been expelled by the British from the Annapolis Valley of mainland Nova Scotia. After the British seized the French settlement of Acadia in 1710, they demanded that the Acadians swear an oath of allegiance to Britain. Most of the Acadians, who had a thriving farming settlement, were not political—more than anything, they wanted to stay apart from the struggles between the French and British empires in North America. A few, however, helped supply the French military fortresses in present-day Nova Scotia and New Brunswick. So, although the vast majority of Acadians had lived peacefully under English rule for decades, the British decided that their presence posed a serious threat and began deporting the Acadians to Europe and to other British colonies. Many of the Acadians who were sent back to France later immigrated to French colonies in

North America. The most sizable portion went to Louisiana, their descendants becoming known as Cajuns. I knew that, but Mary also told me that a small number made their way to Cape Breton Island and settled along its northwestern shore. Walking along in front of these small houses, I was struck by how isolated the Acadian settlers of Chéticamp must have been— probably just a few hundred souls clinging to the sea and the rocky expanses of this mountainous island. What would that have been like? Coming from a rural community of thousands, this handful of families would have depended on each other for everything. But if Chéticamp was isolated, what would Le Buttereau have been like?

As I WALKED around the foundations of Le Buttereau, so crumbled and deteriorated that they looked like stone outcroppings, I tried to picture how the large families survived in such tiny structures. Below the houses were open areas—the remains of farm fields—that stretched down toward the Chéticamp River. It was hard to imagine farming in such a rugged terrain, spending days on the water in flimsy fishing boats, the way the men of these families did. The signs along the path told me that when the waters were open, the men spent Sunday at home in Le Buttereau but returned to fishing shacks in Chéticamp or La Bloque during the week. In winter, the families might cross the frozen river to reach the town in order to buy supplies or, in later years, to go to school. In the warmer months, they would follow a cart path, the remains of which I had been walking, to get to town.

There could never have been many families on this tip of land. In 1936, there were two families named LeBlanc, along with the

Chiassons, the LeBruns and the Deveaus. Each had between nine and eleven children. Fifty people then.

How different my world was. Hundreds of coworkers, hundreds of friends, a neighborhood that stretched unbroken for miles and miles. There were eighty first-grade students at Adam's school. So many people. I thought of Julian's note: Choose the people in your life well. I *could* choose. So many people in the past wouldn't have had that luxury. No real choice, yet so much would have depended on that handful of people they lived among.

The view from the top of Le Chemin du Buttereau was indeed beautiful—the beach and shores curving down below, the blue waters stretching into the distance. But the stunning scenery was only beginning.

An hour later, as I climbed into the highlands in my rental car, the hairpin turns, the plummeting descents and the harrowing rises made me wonder how anyone without a modern six-cylinder vehicle could have made their way around this terrain. It was clear why this part of the world had stayed so sparsely populated. I stopped at numerous lookouts, gazing out across the ocean or looking back at the deep green mountains. I passed the whale museum in Pleasant Bay, making a mental note that I should come back to this place with Adam. I stopped to take a look at Alexander Graham Bell's summer house near Ingonish Centre. I sat for a long time on the beach at Wreck Cove, watching the waves crash against the pebbly shore. It was late afternoon by the time I pulled into Mary and Angus's driveway.

MARY'S DINNER PARTY PROVED TO BE an extraordinary evening. There were mountains of fresh lobster, and after the table had been cleared, the air filled with the sounds of fiddles and harmonicas. Mary and Angus's friends were energetic, engaged, funny, passionate. They talked about everything from politics to art, from world affairs to music. But perhaps my favorite conversation was a quiet one I had with Angus's father before all the guests arrived.

I had offered to help Mary and Angus in the kitchen, but Mary shuffled me out into the living room. "Have a beer with Don," she said. "Angus and I work faster if it's just the two of us."

Don was not a tall man, but he had the solid burliness of someone who spent his life doing physical labor. His hands were veined and calloused, his shoulders slightly stooped, but there was still a sparkle in his green eyes.

I got us each a bottle of beer from the kitchen. (Don's only word was "tch" when I asked him if he wanted a glass.) Then we both retired to the deep living-room chairs and gazed out at the trees before us. Angus had already told me that his father had been a miner, but I was curious to know what that life had been like.

Don seemed delighted to provide the details.

He had gone down into the mines at thirteen.

"My dad, my uncles, those fellas went down when they was ten. By the time I come along they'd raised the age to fourteen. But we needed the money, eh? I wasn't after waiting. I lied about my age, and my dad and his buddies backed me up."

The boys weren't allowed to dig coal. Instead, young Don sat for twelve hours a day, in the pitch black, waiting for a knock on the huge wooden doors that separated the digging areas from the shafts. "I let the miners in. Let them back out with their full carts."

Don said that once you were old enough to dig and haul coal, the days weren't so lonely. Together the men found ways to make the time pass more quickly. They told jokes and stories. They sang together, folk songs and ballads. But the days were still long. In the winter, the miners went down in the dark and came up in the dark.

"Saw the sun only on Sundays, for months and months," Don said with a laugh.

And then there were the "bumps."

"I came through sixteen of them," said Don, running his hand across his forehead. The explosions of coal dust and gases trapped in the mines had taken the lives of many, many of his friends and relatives.

"How did you do it?" I was shaking my head, baffled by the horror of working in the mines.

"Don't get me wrong, b'ye," said Don. Traces of his Gaelic heritage textured his voice. "It was hard work. But it was a good life."

"What do you mean?" I asked. "How can you say that?"

Don was silent for a few seconds. Then he tapped his other hand on the arm of the chair and said, "I don't know that you'd be able to understand it. There's just something about working with a group of fellas, fellas who hold your life in their hands every day. You come through that first explosion, you bring your buddies to the top, you bury others. Someone digs through the coal to find you, to pull you out. Or you sit trapped down there for hours. Maybe ten of you huddled together. When you go back down after the bump, you never look at these guys the same again. You know you have a bond that will never break. You feel lucky. Blessed."

"Wow," I said, still in disbelief. "Even so, I think I'd rather have been a fisherman."

"Blessed Mary and Joseph!" Don burst out. "You wouldn't get me on one of those boats for love or money. You wanna talk about dangerous work. You talk to Joe, Mary's dad."

Don was shaking his head. "Now that's a brave bunch of fellas, I'll tell you that."


ALL DAY I HAD DRIVEN through tiny fishing villages. Mining and fishing—those were essentially the only career choices for generations of men in this corner of the world. And they were communal activities, risky work undertaken by small clusters of souls. In Japan, on one of the most crowded islands in the world, I had been reminded about the importance of treating others well. Here I could see the preciousness of human relationships. Here the people you lived and worked with mattered. Here it could mean life and death.

At first blush, this seemed very different from my life. Other than Adam, who depended on me the way Don had depended on the men in the mines? But then I thought of Juan. Maybe my world wasn't so different after all. There was a moment, maybe more than one, when I had held Juan's life in my hands. And I had not brought him up to the surface.

## Chapter Nine

After my time with Mary and Angus, I flew from Sydney to Halifax, where I spent the night in a hotel. I needed to be at the airport early in the morning for the flight to my next destination—Shanghai. It looked, from the note that Julian had sent, like I would have less than a full day there. My pre-trip self would have thought it an extravagant waste of airfare—flying halfway around the world only to turn around and come back—but I was becoming positively nonchalant about this business of international travel. From my connection in Newark to Shanghai I was able to sleep for a while. I arrived in Shanghai at two in the afternoon (three in the morning Halifax time) and was met by Yu Feng, an earnest young man who announced that he would be my interpreter and guide. He took my bags and hustled me outside the terminal, where a shiny black Bentley was waiting for us. After stowing my luggage, Yu Feng got in the backseat with me.

"Mr. Gao sends his sincerest apologies, but he is in a meeting he could not reschedule. He is hoping that you will meet him at his office at six p.m. He will then take you to his home for dinner. In the meantime, I can show you whatever you would like to see of Shanghai."

I looked at my watch. It had taken me a while to get my luggage and work my way through customs and immigration. I had a few hours I could use to see the city, but the thought of a hot shower and short nap was the most appealing thing I could think of. I thanked Yu Feng for his offer and asked if I could just check into my hotel.

Yu Feng exchanged a few words with our driver, and before I knew it we were speeding into the dense urban landscape of Shanghai.

"Would you care for drink?" Yu Feng asked, pulling on a small door at the back of the seat in front of him. It swung out to reveal a compartment kitted out with a small bar. He then pulled down a tiny table from the leather seat between us.

"Just water," I said. "Thanks." It seemed a pity not to take advantage of this luxury, but I wasn't in the mood for a mixed drink.

We climbed a bridge that stretched across an expanse of dark water. "Huangpu River," said Yu Feng. Then he said, "Mr. Gao's office is downtown, but we have booked you a hotel just a few blocks from the Bund."

I looked at Yu Feng blankly.

Yu Feng explained that the Bund was a broad avenue that

ran along the western bank of the Huangpu River. It was an area where European ex-pats had built many grand buildings during the twenties and thirties.

"Very popular with American and European tourists. Very beautiful at night also," Mr. Yu concluded.

I nodded but didn't say anything. I was thinking about that cascade of hot water and sudsy shampoo.

WHEN I WALKED THROUGH the door of my room, I stopped short and wondered if there had been some sort of mistake. As soon as we had pulled up at the hotel, I knew this would be the most splendid of my accommodations. The lobby, its roof three or four stories high, had black marble floors that gleamed like glass, elegant furnishings and towering palm trees. But hotel lobbies can be a bit deceptive. I've been to places where the lobby looks like a five-star resort, while the rooms remind me of those roadside motels my parents used to pull into on family car trips. So I was expecting a nice room but really wasn't sure.

But this! This was so far beyond "nice" that it left me gasping. I turned to look at Yu Feng, who had insisted on escorting me up. He was frowning and speaking in rapid and angry Mandarin to the bellhop.

"Please accept my humblest apologies," he said to me after he had finished with the unfortunate fellow. "I was just letting him know that there was supposed to be fruit, champagne, a small buffet set out for you in the room. He promises it will all be sent up immediately."

I stood in the foyer of my room, gazing at a space that was substantially bigger than my apartment. I was faced with floor-to-ceiling windows that ran the length of the room. As I moved in, I could see that I not only had a spacious living room, but also a formal dining room. I wandered down the hall to a bedroom that was as big as any hotel room I had ever stayed in. It had its own seating area as well as a study alcove with a desk. The bathroom was a bright, marble-clad wonderland. I walked back into the living room in a daze. Feng looked at me curiously.

"You want to rest. I will leave you now," he said with a little bow of his head. "I shall return at five-thirty to take you to Mr. Gao."

AFTER YU FENG LEFT, I began to explore the suite a little more. In the bathroom, I found a cabinet directly across from the tub. I slid the mahogany door to the side, revealing an enormous television screen. I immediately moved to the bath, turned on the taps and then retreated to the dining room, which had now been set up with the buffet. There I filled a plate with Venezuelan chocolate, Brie cheese, crackers and grapes. Then I uncorked a small bottle of cabernet sauvignon and poured myself a glass. I brought everything into the bathroom on a tray and set the whole business down on the marble ledge that surrounded the huge tub. I located the remote in a small drawer beneath the TV cabinet. I flipped through the movie selections and found one of my favorite action thrillers.

With the Jacuzzi jets pulsing against my body, fine wine and good food filling me with warmth, I soon lost interest in the movie. I used the remote to turn off the television and turn on the sound system. An hour later, I emerged from the tub relaxed, refreshed and marveling at my good fortune. I slipped into a plush cotton robe. As music drifted through the suite, I retrieved my journal and headed into the living room. I stretched out on the deep, soft sectional sofa and opened the journal to a fresh page. *What a great way to live,* I wrote. *I could get used to this!* Then I snapped the book shut.

Yu Feng and the driver picked me up in the Bentley, this time whisking me to Mr. Gao's glittering office tower. After the driver dropped us off, Yu Feng led me through a glass- and fountain-filled lobby, up to the penthouse office.

Yu Feng pushed through the glass doors, and a lovely young woman sitting at reception immediately stood up behind the desk.

"Mr. Yu, Mr. Landry," she said. "I am so sorry. Mr. Gao was certain the meeting would be over by six, but they are still here. I've let Mr. Gao know you have arrived."

Just then a door down the hallway burst open and men began filing out. The sound of loud voices and laughter engulfed them like a wave. As they began to spill into the lobby area, I noticed a familiar face. I thought I was seeing things. And then the voice.

"Mr. Gao, I'm glad you agree with us. I mean, this really is one of the best scripts that's ever been sent to me." It was an actor— a movie star. I'd seen him in dozens of thrillers, the occasional romantic comedy. And he was walking toward me. Beside him was another man I thought I recognized. I couldn't come up with a name, but I had seen him interviewed, or accepting an award or something. A director, maybe; or perhaps a famous producer. And beside them, a tall Asian man who was staring directly at me. He put his hand on the shoulder of the actor, and said something quietly to him. Then he parted from the group and walked over to me.

"Jonathan Landry," the man said, warmly extending his hand. "Gao Li. So sorry to have made you wait. Let me introduce you to some new business partners of mine."

It turned out that Gao Li was a venture capitalist. One of his most recent investments was in a new Hollywood production company started by a group that included the actor and the other man—a director, I learned. They had been signing the final papers in that day's meeting.

"You're in for a real treat," the actor said to me. He was smiling and thumping Mr. Gao on the back.

People say that when you meet famous people, they are smaller than you'd expect. But this guy was every bit as tall and muscled as he looked on the big screen. His clothes were casual, but they didn't look like anything I owned. I wondered if that was what designer clothes looked like, if truly expensive shirts and jeans just had a certain flash to them. Sunglasses were perched on his forehead. It looked as if they had been there all day, clinging to his temples, ready to slide down over his eyes in case he needed to go incognito in a hurry.

"Get Mr. Gao to take you to his yacht," the actor was saying to me. He gestured toward Gao Li. "What a party we had there last night. Crazy. Seriously, Mr. Gao, she is one beautiful boat. And you throw one hell of a bash. Thanks. Thanks for everything." As Gao Li and the actor shook hands, a serious-looking young man leaned toward Mr. Gao, speaking quietly.

Gao Li then said, "Gentlemen, the helicopter is here. Shall we head up?" Then he turned to me.

"Jonathan, would you like to join me to see my friends off?"

I had never before been to a helipad. We headed through a door on the other side of the penthouse and took an elevator just one floor up. The doors opened onto the wide, flat roof. There, some distance away, was a helicopter, its blades spinning. It was a surreal feeling—to stand on top of a building, over a hundred stories off the ground, the air rushing above our heads, a strangely open sky stretching into the distance. The rooftops of other skyscrapers looked like floating platforms dotting the concrete canyon that surrounded us.

The actor, the director and another couple of men bent over and started a slow run to the helicopter. They looked as if they did this sort of thing every day. Once they climbed on board and settled themselves, the chopper began to lift away slowly from the building. Gao Li and I waved. I could see the actor at the window waving back. Then Mr. Gao and I headed down to the office.

"I am sorry that I couldn't send the helicopter to bring you from the airport, but I'm afraid we needed to do another safety check for this flight today, so the timing did not work."

I didn't know what to say. It hadn't occurred to me that I might have the benefit of this sort of transportation.

As we rode the elevator and made our way to Mr. Gao's office, my thoughts raced. Gao Li's life was rewriting all my standards of luxury. I had never ridden in a Bentley before, but it was now something I might long for. And a driver. Then there was the suite at the hotel, this swanky office, the helicopter. And the actor. How glamorous was that? It all reminded me of the grand plan I had formulated after high school.

LIKE SO MANY KIDS, I found high school and the teen years something of a trial. It wasn't because I was unpopular, or struggled in school, or was plagued by some deep insecurity. Instead, my adolescent self existed in a relentless state of dissatisfaction. While I knew there were plenty of kids who had things worse than I did, all I could really see were those who seemed to have it better. When spring break or the summer holidays came around, I made a mental list of the kids who were setting off on fabulous holidays—the Caribbean or ski trips in March, a cottage or Europe in July. I noticed who had the best bike, the newest ice skates, the most spending money. I made note of the houses they lived in and the cars their parents drove. And the kids who had their own cars—their good fortune was like a flashing neon sign above a shop I couldn't enter. I decided during those covetous years that I wasn't going to accept my parents' life of coupon-cutting, second-hand vehicles and low-rent vacations. I was going to make big money when I finished college. And I was going to live in style.

Of course, there's nothing like a little reality to make you recalibrate your expectations. But while I hadn't managed to buy a Bentley, I had acquired a house considerably bigger than the one I grew up in, and I had been working my way up the corporate ladder toward a more luxurious life. During this trip for Julian, however, I had been loosening my grip on that goal. I was beginning to question some of my priorities and to look at the "good life" in a whole new light. This visit was reminding me of why I had set myself those targets in the first place. Gao Li's life looked pretty great. There was just no getting around it. Unlike Julian, I had no Ferrari to sell. But was I ready to sell my *dream* of a Ferrari?

Gao Li led me into his office. It was, of course, an enormous corner suite with wraparound windows. Antique lacquered furniture punctuated the room. In one corner was what appeared to be a silk brocade couch and chairs; in another, an extravagant ebony desk. A bottle of champagne sat in an ice bucket on the coffee table in front of us.

"Left over from the meeting," Gao Li said, looking at it. "Would you care for a glass or shall we head to my home for a drink before dinner?"

As much as I would have liked to linger in that elegant place, sipping champagne and gazing at the Shanghai skyline, I was even more curious to see where—and how—Gao Li lived.

"I'd be happy to head out," I said.

"Very good," Gao Li replied. "I am a little anxious to get home myself. I've been busy the last few days entertaining the production company people, and I am missing my home and my wife and daughter."

"Ah yes, I heard about the yacht," I said.

"Yes, I hope you don't mind that I can't take you on a ride this trip," said Gao Li. "Julian tells me your time is limited, and the crew is still cleaning up from last night."

"No worries," I said, perhaps with too much insistence. I *was* a little disappointed not to see a trophy that had impressed a Hollywood giant who no doubt had been on his share of good-sized yachts.

Gao Li walked over to his desk and pressed a button on his phone.

"Yang Jing-we," he said into the speaker, "can you have Sung Hao bring my car around? Jonathan and I are ready to leave." Then he turned to me.

"I brought my own car this morning since I wanted to keep the company car and driver free to take you around today."

As we headed down the elevator to the lobby, I found myself wondering what kind of car a fellow like Gao Li would choose. Would he go for a sedan like a Mercedes, or would he have a sportier vehicle? Maybe a Maserati or a Porsche? Perhaps a Lamborghini. Or even a Ferrari.

As we pushed out the glass lobby doors I scanned the cars lined up along the sidewalk. There was a Lexus, an Alfa Romeo, a BMW and an Aston Martin. My money was on the Aston Martin. I almost began walking in that direction when I heard Gao Li say, "Over here, Jonathan." He was walking in the opposite direction, toward a man in a livery uniform who was holding a set of keys. The man was standing beside a Volvo station wagon.

"Thank you, Sung Hao," Gao Li said, taking the keys and walking around to the driver's side of the Volvo.

I realized that I had been standing on the sidewalk, watching Gao Li, my mouth slightly open, my feet frozen in place. I snapped my jaw closed and stepped quickly toward the passenger side. I opened the door and was about to sit down, but a magazine was on the seat.

"Sorry about that," said Gao Li, picking up the magazine and tossing it in the backseat. "My daughter's."

I was so surprised by the car that I didn't say anything as Gao Li pulled out into traffic. This was, after all, the kind of car my neighbors drove, the type that lined the parking lot at Adam's soccer games. There was nothing wrong with it, but it wasn't the sort of vehicle that I thought a man with Mr. Gao's obvious resources would drive.

We were moving on and off major roads, through seas of high-rise offices and apartment buildings. At every turn, I expected a break, a move into low-rise suburbia or even a stretch of green space, but the line of dense buildings went on and on and on. Gao Li and I chatted amiably. He told me about some of his big ventures, including the production company and a new enterprise he was funding in Brazil. I told him about my work in the auto industry. Eventually I asked how he knew Julian.

"We met in court. While he was suing me," Gao Li said with a chuckle. "Actually, his client was suing me," Mr. Gao continued. "Unsuccessfully, I might add."

"I thought Julian never lost," I said. I had heard the stories.

"His client didn't have a case, but for Julian that usually didn't matter. I was just lucky that the suit was at the end of Julian's legal career—when he wasn't exactly at the top of his game."

"Let me guess," I said. "He got in touch with you again after his return from the Himalayas."

"You are not mistaken," said Gao Li, who was slowing down before pulling into a rare parking space along the side of the street.

"Please excuse me," said Gao Li. "I just want to stop in at the coffee shop right there. I'll only be a minute."

I watched as Gao Li got out of the car, ran down the sidewalk, and disappeared into a small, brightly lit café. It was now at least eight in the evening, and the place looked packed. I could see dozens of people clustered tightly around small tables, stretching back into the narrow shop.

As he promised, Gao Li came out just a minute later. When he got into the car, he looked pleased.

"Another one of my investments," he said. "Mr. Chang is

from my hometown. He started here in Shanghai with a little cart in the corridor of a shopping mall. I paid for half the cart. And now his café is one of the most popular spots in this part of the city. We are talking about opening a second location."

"It seems to be doing pretty well," I said.

"Well, certainly in the evenings it is. That's when people go out for coffee here—afternoons and evenings. Coffee isn't a morning thing in China yet. But Chang Ning is working on that. He has a few morning regulars. And he's trying to reach out to the older crowd. Right now, his clients are mostly young. Some business-people, but most people my age still see coffee as a Western fad."

Gao Li turned his attention to the road, while I watched the little shop disappear behind us in the rearview mirror. It seemed like an awfully small enterprise for a man who was playing at Gao Li's level.

Another twenty minutes passed before we were turning off the busy street into an underground parking garage. The change in direction had startled me. We were surrounded by non-descript high-rise apartment buildings. I hadn't seen anything that looked liked luxury condos or a wealthy urban enclave.

Gao Li pulled into a parking spot. The cars on either side of him were modest. Gao Li got out and opened the back door to retrieve the magazine and his briefcase. I followed him as he headed to a bank of elevators.

MR. GAO'S APARTMENT, like the car, was in striking con-trast to everything I had seen earlier in the day. It was consider-ably bigger than my apartment to be sure, and the furnishings were certainly elegant and tasteful. It was on the fiftieth floor, so the view of the Shanghai skyline at night was breathtaking. But everything else about the place was simple. His wife, Gao Ling, a pretty middle-aged woman, was dressed in dark jeans and a white shirt—something Annisha might wear—with bright turquoise jewelry. There were no diamonds weighing down her fingers or dripping from her ears.

Their daughter, Gao Mei, was out with friends, so it was just the three of us for dinner. Mr. Gao and I had a glass of wine, while Mrs. Gao brought various things to the table.

"May I help?" I asked, moving into the dining room.

"No, no," said Gao Ling. "Thank you."

The table was filling with covered dishes. The smell was heavenly.

"Did you cook all this yourself?" I asked in amazement.

Mr. Gao started to speak in Mandarin to his wife. My host was so fluent in English that it hadn't occurred to me that Gao Ling might not be as well.

"My wife likes to cook," said Gao Li. "If we have a big party, we will hire caterers, but when it is just the three of us, or a few friends for dinner, she prefers to prepare everything. Sometimes she even lets me help." Mr. Gao laughed, and Gao Ling shot him a questioning look. He repeated his comment in Mandarin, and she smiled.

I ATE FAR MORE than I should have. When the meal was done, Gao Li and I helped clear the table and then he suggested that we drink our tea in his study.

"I have something to give you," he said, leading the way.

We moved into a small room lined with bookshelves. A desk

was moved up against the window, the seat facing out toward the brightly lit city. Two deep upholstered chairs and a round coffee table filled the rest of the space.

I sat in one of the chairs while Gao Li went to the desk. He opened a drawer and pulled out something. When he turned back toward me he was holding a small, red, silk-covered box.

"Julian's talisman," he said proudly, placing the box carefully in my hand.

I lifted the lid and peered inside. The box held a small cylindrical shell—about two inches long and half an inch wide. I tipped it out of the box into my hand. A plain, ordinary seashell. It really didn't look like an amulet or any kind of special treasure. A small piece of folded paper was wedged into the bottom of the box. I worked it out and unfolded it.

The note read:

*Life's simplest pleasures are life's greatest joys.*

*Most people don't discover what's most important in life until they are too old to do anything about it. They spend many of their best years pursuing things that matter little in the end. While society invites us to fill our lives with material objects, the best part of us knows that the more basic pleasures are the ones that enrich and sustain us. No matter how easy or hard our current conditions, we all have a wealth of simple blessings around us—waiting to be counted. As we do, our happiness grows. Our gratitude expands. And each day becomes a breathtaking gift.*

I looked up at Gao Li. All the trappings of wealth I had seen this afternoon, and then the simple apartment, the unassuming car.

"I imagine that you have more to say about this," I said, holding up the shell.

"Yes, I have some thoughts about this talisman and Julian's note. But first, I think you have some questions for me."

I cocked my head. I wasn't sure what Gao Li was getting at.

"I noticed your expression when you saw my car and the apartment. And I think you may be wondering about that coffee shop, too. You were just too polite to ask. But don't worry about offending me. Ask your questions."

I was clearly not fooling Mr. Gao—he already knew what perplexed me. But he wanted me to put it into words, so I would have to try.

"It's just the yacht, the Bentley, the helicopter. I mean, it looks like your business is doing extremely well, but. . ." Now I was in trouble. I couldn't think of any good way to put this. "I'm not trying to be rude, but your car, your apartment. I mean they're nice, they're perfectly nice, but. . ."

"But they are not the car and the home of a truly wealthy man," said Gao Li, smiling. "You are wondering if I am trying to create the illusion of success for my business. You are wondering if I am struggling financially."

I didn't say anything. This was awkward.

"No, Jonathan. I am not struggling. The signs of wealth you saw today are all very real. I am an extremely rich man. But my car, my home, it all goes back to that little piece of paper you are holding." I looked down at Julian's note.

"The Volvo is a simple pleasure?" I asked.

Gao Li laughed. "Maybe for someone else, but I don't really care about cars," said Mr. Gao. "No," he continued, "I guess the connection takes a bit of explaining. You see, Jonathan, I was not born into wealth. My family wasn't even middle-class. Not by North American standards, in any case. My father and mother both worked in a garment factory in Xintang. The tiny apartment we lived in would make this one look like a mansion."

I could feel my face growing red. I began to realize that I had applied to Gao Li all sorts of assumptions and drawn conclusions formulated during my middle-class life.

"I am not trying to make you feel embarrassed, Jonathan. I am trying to gently explain all the contradictions you have seen today."

I nodded.

"To tell you the story of how I got from the Xintang factories to here would take all evening, so I'll just say that I managed to get out of there and start a small business here in Shanghai. I worked hard, I was lucky, and eventually I sold that business for what seemed like a king's ransom to me. With that money, I began to invest in other companies, large and small. There has been no shortage of opportunities in this country over the past few decades."

Gao Li explained that when his business began to take off, he did what I would have assumed any newly wealthy man would do. He bought expensive clothes, fancy cars and a yacht. He spent lavishly on dining out, vacations and gifts.

"The only thing I didn't do was buy a glitzy penthouse apartment or a huge house. My wife wouldn't hear of it. We got this place before our daughter was born. To Gao Ling, it was home. She never wanted to move."

Mr. Gao went on to say that one day his wife had asked him to take her and their daughter for an afternoon stroll through the park. He told her that he didn't have time—he was off to a car dealership to check out a sports car he was interested in buying. Gao Ling looked at him with disappointment and asked, "You would rather shop than live?"

"She wasn't angry, just sad. All afternoon, I could hear the echo of her words. And I kept hearing it for days, weeks."

Gao Li didn't buy the new car. He realized that he didn't care at all about cars. And he didn't care about having a fashionable place to live. In fact, he didn't enjoy most of the objects he was spending so much of his time acquiring.

"I was buying them just because that is what I thought I should do. So I stopped shopping. And I didn't miss the things one bit. What I did regret was missing out on that walk."

Gao Li said he kept the Bentley and the helicopter for business purposes. The helicopter saved him a lot of time—time that he could spend with his family. And the yacht was a good place to entertain because his home was too small for that.

"That's where the wisdom of the talisman comes in," said Gao Li. "I realized that by living a certain way, I was missing out on simple pleasures, life's *greatest* ones."

"Money can't buy happiness, right?" I said. That was one of my mother's favorite chestnuts.

"Don't get me wrong," said Gao Li now, leaning forward earnestly. "I've been poor, so I would never say that money is not important. You have been enjoying Shanghai's opulence today. But what you haven't had a chance to see is the considerable poverty that exists in this country. The poor here—the poor everywhere—have fewer choices. They can't always enjoy the simple things because they are working so hard to stave off hunger and suffering. They are too exhausted from the difficult work of feeding and clothing and sheltering themselves and

their families. My parents had very little time for pleasure—
simple or otherwise."

Gao Li sat back again. Then he bent forward to refill his tea-
cup. He offered to fill mine, but I shook my head.

"You know, Jonathan," Gao Li said slowly, "it seems to me
that most of us who are lucky enough to escape poverty forget
what having a little money does. It frees us to make choices
about our careers, where we live, things like that. It frees us to
spend time with friends and family. It allows us to enjoy the
simple things. But people think that money is only about what
can be bought, what is consumed. So they become distracted
by the next shiny toy, just like I did. And if they start buying too
much stuff, spending too much, they can get trapped. Almost
more trapped than the truly poor. They become beholden to
mortgages and credit card debt and loans. Or just trapped by
having to make the big money their lifestyle depends on. After
all, as Julian always says, the more addicted you are to *having*,
the less devoted you will be to *becoming*. And what I've discovered is that real happiness doesn't come from accumulating
things. No, lasting happiness comes from learning how to savor
common pleasures like a cool breeze on a hot day, or a star-
filled sky after a day of hard work. Or laughter with loved ones
over a three-hour-long home-cooked meal."

"The shell," I said, lifting it back out of the box. "Collecting
shells on a beach?"

"Exactly," he said. "One of the best times I have ever had was
building sand castles with my wife and daughter at the beach in
Qingdao. The shell that Julian gave me has served beautifully to
remind me of the perfect moments of that perfect day. And those
memories are a form of wealth."

We were both quiet for a moment. I was thinking of another beach, another woman, another child. But something was still nagging at me.

Finally I said, "But Gao Li, if you are now a wealthy man, why not just quit? Spend all your time on the simple pleasures."

He laughed. "Good question," he said. "My wife asks me that all the time."

He took a sip of tea and then placed his cup back down on the table in front of us.

"Work is also a pleasure for me, Jonathan. But it's more than that. Remember that coffee shop we stopped at?"

I nodded.

"That's not the only small business I have invested in. For every large venture I undertake, I try to find at least two small businesses to support. I look for people who think they can change their own lives as well as the lives of others. Small businesses in country villages and crowded cities; family enterprises and individual college students; entrepreneurs with ideas and a heart. And I follow these little businesses like traders follow the market swings. The men and women I give money to turn my dollars into new lives—they extend my help farther than I would be able to do on my own. And they help me build a better world in the process. Making a difference has now become more important to me than making money. This realization has made my life so much more joyful, Jonathan."

"That's amazing," I said. Mr. Gao's story made me feel humble.

Gao Li shook his head. Then he looked over at the window, at the brilliant lights of Shanghai spread out before us. I didn't say anything. He seemed to be thinking about something.

Eventually Gao Li started again.

"A few months after Julian had his heart attack, he wrote me a letter," he said. "I have to tell you, I wasn't sure I wanted to open it. I was afraid that it might be another lawsuit. But it wasn't. It was a handwritten note. Julian said he had quit his practice, had sold all his belongings. He had traveled. He had learned things. And he said that he was very glad he had lost the suit against me. He said I was a man he would like to get to know better."

Gao Li was smiling at the memory. "I will never forget the closing lines of that letter," he continued. "'Lasting happiness,' Julian wrote, 'comes from the size of our impact, not the extent of our income. Real fulfillment is a product of the value we create and the contribution we make, not of the car we drive or the house we buy. And I've learned that self-worth is more important than net worth. But I think you know that already, Gao Li.'"

"And you did," I agreed.

"And I did," said Gao Li.

LATER THAT NIGHT, back at my hotel, I stood at the living-room windows and gazed out at the skyline across the river. The view was marvelous during the day, but after sunset the skyline took on the look of some fantastic futuristic amusement park or an elaborate display of abstract sculpture—spectacularly colored spheres, columns, spires, cylinders, gleaming and sparkling like electrified crystal. Even driving back to my hotel from Gao Li's place had been a wonder. The city skyline crowded with jewel-toned light. I had never seen anything like it.

But I thought of what Mr. Gao had said to me that evening. All this glitter was seductive. I would have loved to spend more time here to explore the city, but the feelings Gao Li's office, the Bentley, the helicopter, the actor, even this hotel suite had evoked in me were more about pleasure than real happiness. Maybe that was the key distinction Gao Li had been trying to make. How could I expect these kinds of riches to make me happy when I had been finding it impossible to enjoy even the simple joys of my life? It seemed to me that both Julian and Gao Li had found something that most very rich people will never have: a feeling that they have enough.

The truth was, right now, here alone in my hotel room, thousands of miles from home, if I could have any one thing, it wouldn't be a yacht or a fancy car or a sprawling mansion. It would be an answer.

I DREAMED THAT NIGHT of the curving Cape Breton roads I had driven earlier that week. They had made me think of Juan, made me think of his last moments. He lived outside the city, and he was driving home in the evening, the rush hour long over. It was a spring night; the roads were dry. He was on a stretch of highway that ran through wooded areas near his home. It was a route he drove every day, yet somehow he had crashed through a steel barrier and plummeted into a ravine. The medical investigator said that he had suffered multiple life-threatening injuries, but that the cause of death was a massive heart attack. Emily, his wife, said that work stress had led to his death. I had no doubt about that. By the time he climbed into his car that night, Juan was a gray specter of the man I once knew. The last few years at work—the pressure, the isolation, the abandonment by friends and colleagues—that had destroyed him. But there was one question that no one was asking. One question that haunted me. One question I desperately wanted answered. But it was a puzzle for which I might never find the solution.

# CHAPTER TEN

NOTHING COULD HAVE BEEN more in contrast with Shanghai's glitzy, frenetic cityscape than the quiet, dusty expanses that spread out around me as I traveled the highway between Phoenix and Sedona, Arizona. After being in the air for the better part of the day, I had arrived in Phoenix in the early afternoon, picked up a rental car and headed out. Despite the fact that I had been moving back and forth between time zones like an airline pilot, I felt remarkably good. I didn't think jetlag was something you were supposed to get used to, but I now seemed able to fall asleep when I needed to and to get up with the sun, wherever I was.

In a suburb on the northern edge of Phoenix, I pulled into a restaurant that was part of those ubiquitous chains that offer quantity over quality. I was hungry, and this would be fast and easy. As I walked inside, I noticed a display of tourist pamphlets against the wall of the doorway. I plucked a few out of the rack before I headed to the hostess desk.

The hostess showed me to a table, and a young man, no older than seventeen I would guess, materialized at my side. I ordered a club sandwich and some juice, and the waiter disappeared again. I looked over at the small pile of pamphlets I'd dropped on the table. One in particular had caught my eye. It was about "vortex tours" you could do in and around Sedona. According to the pamphlet, the Sedona area is thought to be the location of at least four energy vortices—places in the landscape where the Earth's invisible lines of energy intersect to create a concentration of power that could have extraordinary therapeutic properties. There seemed to be quite the cottage industry associated with these vortices: one pamphlet listed dozens of massage specialists, tarot readers, personal magnetic-field re-balancers, even past-life regression therapists. *Oh brother,* I thought. I was having enough challenges with *this* life without diving into another.

I wondered why Julian had sent the talisman out this way. Did the talisman have something to do with crystals or auras or energy fields?

By the time I had finished my sandwich, my young server was at my side, offering coffee and dessert. I declined but couldn't help thinking about how much this young man reminded me of Lluis. He might not spend the rest of his days waiting tables, but I had a feeling that whatever he ended up doing, he'd do with enthusiasm and success.

I paid my bill, left the restaurant and crossed the parking lot to the rental car. It was time to head out to meet Ronnie

Begay. According to Julian's directions, she lived about a hundred miles north of Phoenix.

After a few minutes on the highway, I rolled down the windows. The dry desert air felt good against my skin—a welcome change from the steaminess of Shanghai. I heard my phone beep but didn't pick it up. I had to pay attention to the road.

The number of messages from the office had dwindled steadily. I hadn't really expected to hear any more from Tessa, but Nawang had been quiet, too. Yesterday, she acknowledged this absence with an apology: *Sorry I haven't been keeping you up to date on everything, but it's been crazy around here. For the past few days, Luke, Katherine and Sven have been holed up in the conference room with a group of men and women I don't recognize. Rumor is that there will be an announcement by the end of the day, maybe tomorrow. No doubt a merger is under way, but everyone is trying to figure out if they are buying us or we are buying them. David is freaking out. He seems fairly convinced that he is going to be given his walking papers either way.*

I tried not to feel happy about that. Ayame would not be impressed by my mean-spirited reaction.

*I don't know what to think about my position—or yours,* Nawang wrote.

I realized that the uncertainty didn't worry me at all.

The inevitable reorganization at work would not be a threat to me. It would be an opportunity. If I got a severance package, I would use the freedom to talk with companies that might be able to offer me a position that suited me better. If the reconfigured company wanted to keep me on, I would see if there might be other places in the firm for me. Since Juan's death, there had been a vacancy in the design department. Maybe I would see about that. Either way, I could use the shifting business to my advantage. I felt excited about the prospect of change.

That was something new: looking at change without fear; or maybe not completely without fear, but with an acceptance of the fear that always came with any sort of significant upheaval in my life. Maybe I was becoming more like my sister, Kira.

While I always chose the safe, obvious path, Kira had struck out on her own route again and again. After high school, she worked for half a year and then joined a youth exchange program, doing volunteer work at a number of orphanages. After college, she traveled the world, visiting marvelous destinations—from Malaysia, Bali and New Zealand to Sweden, Estonia and Russia—working here and there to support herself. During one of her journeys she visited a women's cooperative in Guatemala. She was impressed with the things the women made—elaborately embroidered and decorated cushions and linens—and with the industry, hope and courage of the women themselves. When she came back home, Kira announced that she was going to find a market for the women's products and help them sell their wares. Just a few years later, she was running a hugely successful fair-trade importing business and had storefronts in half a dozen major North American cities. When her twins were born, Kira decided to sell her business to one of her partners. She would take a few years at home and plan out her next career venture. When I expressed surprise that she could give up the enterprise she had worked so hard for, she just laughed. "I'm not going to live the same day over and over again, and call it a life," she said.

JULIAN'S DRIVING INSTRUCTIONS were simple enough. I turned off the highway, onto a small road about an hour and a half after I had set off. The road wound around until I came to a smattering of houses strung out along either side. Most were mobile homes, decked out with porches and awnings and other not-so-mobile additions. Interspersed among them were a few small, low bungalows. A number were set off by chain-link fences. Small patches of brown grass surrounded the houses, but the desert crawled right up to the edge of the struggling turf and stretched back away for miles. Eventually I spotted the street number on a mailbox that stood in front of a neat brown home. I pulled into the gravel drive, alongside a gray pickup truck parked in front of a small garage. As I climbed out of the car into the midday heat, I noticed that the front yard was festooned with various bits of brightly colored extruded plastic— children's toys. No doubt the sound of the crunching gravel alerted Ronnie, who had swung the front door open just as I was stepping up to it.

"Jonathan!" she said, as if we were long-lost friends.

Ronnie was probably about sixty—her hair, which had some dark streaks, was mostly a silvery gray. Her bronzed face was lined, but not at all drawn. When she laughed, it looked almost as if the creases around her eyes and mouth were dancing.

She ushered me into the living room, cautioning me to watch my step around the toys and games that were scattered across the floor.

"Can you believe I cleaned this up once already this morning?" she laughed.

"I have a six-year-old," I said. "I know how it goes."

Ronnie moved into the kitchen and peered out the window. I

followed her gaze. In the backyard were a half-dozen children of various sizes playing some sort of game with a large inflatable ball. Ronnie told me they were her grandkids and her grand-nephews.

The grandchildren were visiting for the afternoon, but the grandnephews were permanent residents.

"My niece," said Ronnie matter-of-factly, "has been in and out of trouble since I can remember. Her father isn't in the picture; her mother isn't well and has never been able to help out. A few years back, things reached a crisis point. It looked like her kids were going to be taken away."

Ronnie was now opening the kitchen window, calling out.

"Rose, make sure that Sammy gets a turn, okay?"

Then she turned back to me.

"José and I were the only ones in the family with the room and the resources to take the kids in." Ronnie put her hand on her chest, as if she were pressing her heart back in.

"Best decision I made in my life," she said with a smile.

Ronnie went to the fridge and took out a large jug.

"Iced tea?" she asked. When I nodded, she filled two glasses that were sitting on the counter and handed one to me. She left the other on the counter and moved toward the back door.

"Sorry," she said, "but I promised the kids a snack, and I'd better get to it before I ruin their appetites for dinner." Ronnie went out the door. I watched her through the screen as she headed into the garage. She came back a few minutes later with an enormous watermelon. When the children spotted it, they followed her into the kitchen, whooping and hollering. "Watermelon, watermelon, watermelon," they chanted, as if calling for an encore at a rock concert.

"First of the season," Ronnie said to me. "I know you can get it now at the grocery store any time of the year, but I never buy it until the hot weather really hits. It just tastes so much better in the heat."

She told the children to go outside to the picnic bench, and she would bring them their snack when it was ready. The kids filed out the door.

Ronnie placed the watermelon on a large wooden cutting board on the kitchen counter, took an enormous knife from a drawer and plunged it into the center of the melon. It made a satisfying *thwack*. Ronnie pulled the knife down through the wet fruit, cutting it in half and in half again. Then she began to slice each quarter as if she were slicing a dense loaf of bread. When she had cut up the first quarter, she picked up a middle slice and held it out to me.

I couldn't remember the last time I had watermelon, but when I bit into the cool, sweet flesh I felt a rush of memory sweep over me. Another backyard, so many decades ago. My mother, her hair tied back in a bright scarf, a tray proffered in her outstretched arms.

This was the kind of thing Gao Li had been talking about. Here, at Ronnie's house, the first watermelon of the season was still an event, a cause for celebration.

After Ronnie had taken a huge plate outside and then made a second trip to gather up the rinds and wipe a few faces, she returned and finally took a long pull from her iced tea.

"Hope you don't mind," she said, "but now I've got to start dinner."

I sat in Ronnie's air-conditioned kitchen as she set about preparing the family meal. Her daughter Rose would probably stay with the kids, she said. Ronnie's husband, José, would be home soon. He might bring his sister with him. They worked together.

"My house is never empty," said Ronnie. "It can be exhausting, but I like it this way."

She went to the fridge and pulled out a large bag of red peppers. As she washed them, she looked back over her shoulder at me.

"But I have something to give you, and it would be nice to have someplace quiet to talk. I thought that after supper we could drive out to the Red Rocks so you can see the sunset. You can't come all this way without seeing it."

SEVERAL HOURS LATER Ronnie and I were sitting on the edge of a massive boulder, staring at the striking red sandstone pillars that rose majestically out of the desert. As the sun dipped, the rocks seemed to take on its fading fire. They were glowing bright orange like embers. The scene reminded me a bit of the Temple of the Magician in the morning sun.

"I feel like I've seen this before," I said.

"The movies," said Ronnie. "Westerns."

Yeah, I thought, that was probably it. But it felt special here somehow. As if I had a more personal connection to the place. I wondered if that had anything to do with what I had seen in the pamphlets.

"I was reading a little bit about those vortices," I said to Ronnie. She winced.

"We call them 'vortexes' around here," she said.

"Vortexes. Right. Are we close to them? Are any around here?" I asked.

"There's one a couple of miles that way." Ronnie waved her hand to the right, but didn't offer any other details.

"You don't sound as if you put much stock in that stuff," I said to her.

Ronnie smiled and dug at the hard-packed earth with the toe of her shoe.

"Well," she said slowly, "Native people in these parts never considered those spots particularly sacred—or at least they don't think of them as any *more* sacred than the rest of the land."

Ronnie bent down to brush the dirt from her shoe. "But that's not to say this place isn't special. My people have always had a connection to the land, and I believe in the healing powers of the earth. Of being one with nature."

"But. . ." I said. There was clearly a "but" on its way.

"But," said Ronnie. She was gazing back at the rocks now. The light was getting a little weaker. The rocks were glowing softly. "I really believe that the most powerful healing is anywhere people are. It isn't confined to a place or a time or a circumstance."

A small gray lizard scurried across the ground in front of us. I watched it disappear behind some brush.

"Did Julian ever tell you how we met?" Ronnie asked.

"No," I said, "but I bet there's a story."

And there was. Ronnie told me that she had met Julian many years ago, when he was a high-flying lawyer. "Well, I didn't know what he did then," she admitted. "He told me later."

Julian was driving down the highway one late afternoon, on his way to see these very rocks that Ronnie and I were gazing at now. He was on a golfing junket in Phoenix, and he had rented a sleek sports car for his stay. He and a beautiful female friend had headed out with a loaf of bread, some cheese and an enormous thermos of martinis. They were going to have a picnic by the rocks as the sun went down. But before they had even reached the town of Sedona, their car broke down. Ronnie saw the bright yellow sports car parked at the side of the road, steam pouring out from under its hood. She pulled over and offered to give Julian and his companion a ride. Ronnie drove the two of them back to her place, where they called the rental company. It would send a tow truck and try to deliver another vehicle to her house.

"That, I don't mind telling you, was a long afternoon," said Ronnie.

"My house was full as usual—my teenage children, my nieces and nephews. It was noisy. José was playing his guitar; the kids were laughing and shouting—jumping on the trampoline we had out back."

Julian and his friend had chatted a little with Ronnie and her husband, but they were clearly annoyed that their plans had been so thoroughly derailed. And the busyness of the household, Ronnie could tell, was wearing on their nerves.

"The young woman, whose name I can't remember, couldn't stop tapping her foot. And Julian kept sneaking gulps from the thermos while he peered out the front window every two seconds. Since the two of them didn't really want to talk, José, the kids and I just continued on with our day."

When the new rental car showed up several hours later, Ronnie had to insist that Julian's friend drive it back to the city since Julian was in no condition.

"And that was the last I thought of either of them for a long, long while," said Ronnie.

Then, several years later, she received a call from Julian. He had to remind her who he was. He took her by surprise by asking if he could come for a visit. He said he wanted to see the Red Rocks finally. Mostly, however, he wanted to talk with Ronnie.

"When he got here, well, I tell you, I wouldn't have recognized him," Ronnie said. "He looked younger, somehow. Even taller, too, if that's possible. And he seemed peaceful. So peaceful and happy. That wasn't the man I remembered."

Julian told Ronnie that he had just come back from the Himalayas, where he had spent time with a group of monks. The lessons they shared had turned his life around. But what he learned also made him look at people differently. And he came to realize that many people he crossed paths with over the years had much to teach him, much to share.

Ronnie and Julian had gone to see the Red Rocks in the setting sun, just as she and I had done. The two of them had walked for a while, the rocks glowing in the distance. The quiet and tranquillity seemed such a stark contrast to the noise and energy of Ronnie's household. To her, this contrast only made both places seem more special.

As they took one last look at the rocks and the sun slipped from the sky, Julian turned to Ronnie.

"You," he said, "I think you know the secret of life. If I asked you, what is the purpose of it all, what would you say?"

Ronnie stopped telling her story for a moment. I looked over at her.

"Do you know the secret of life?" I asked in wonder.

"It was so odd that Julian asked me that question," said

Ronnie, shaking her head. "You know my mother belonged to the Hopi tribe, my father was a Navajo. Their peoples share many beliefs, but there are differences. I was raised with those traditional Native beliefs. But my husband is Catholic. We have friends who are Jewish, Buddhist, Muslim. I have tried to learn a little about all these faiths. In my youth, I spent a lot of time studying, talking to people."

The sky was getting dark now; the rocks that loomed on the horizon had darkened to a deep red. Ronnie looked out in the distance, but she seemed lost in thought. I waited for her to start talking again.

"I spent a lot of time looking for answers. But in the end I decided that, while there were many truths, it all came down to one simple thing."

I looked at Ronnie expectantly. I realized that I was holding my breath.

"The purpose of life, Jonathan, is *love*. It's that simple."

I was quiet a moment, letting that sink in.

"If you're not loved, nothing else matters?" I asked.

"Not quite," said Ronnie. "The purpose of life is *to love*. Love is a verb. And it has to be at the center of your universe. It should drive everything you do. I don't think you can be truly alive if you do not love."

That is what Ronnie had told Julian. Julian had replied that the monks agreed with her.

"In fact," Julian told her, "they said pretty much the same thing to me, but I traveled all the way to the Himalayas to hear that message, when I could have just heard it from you all those years ago."

"You weren't ready to hear," Ronnie told Julian. "I could have said it a thousand ways, and you wouldn't have heard it."

Ronnie had finished her story. She was digging in her pocket now, pulling out a small woven bag.

"The talisman," she said, handing it to me.

I opened the small braided drawstring and tipped the contents into my hand. The talisman was a tiny silver heart. It looked handmade, its polished surfaces round and smooth. I rolled the heart in my fingers. I had been holding the little bag upside down, and now a small slip of paper I hadn't seen fell from it. Ronnie bent down and picked it up.

She handed it to me.

*The Purpose of Life Is to Love*
*How well you live comes down to how much you love. The heart is wiser than the head. Honor it. Trust it. Follow it.*

Ronnie and I walked slowly back to where we'd parked. There was a crispness in the air now, and a fragrant desert wind blew softly. We climbed into Ronnie's truck without saying a word and began moving down the road, the sound of the tires echoing around us.

Ronnie and I were silent on the drive back to her house. She seemed to recognize that I needed some time to reflect. I was realizing that I had been focusing most of my thoughts about my "authentic life" on my job. I was in the wrong job. That had been clear almost since the beginning of the trip. But Ayame, Mary, and now Ronnie had helped me to see that I'd betrayed myself within my personal life as well. I had not been true to myself in my friendships, with my family, or in my love life. If I had been the kind of friend I valued, I wouldn't have turned my back on Juan. If I had focused on being the parent I wanted to be, I wouldn't have skimped on time with Adam. And if I had been true to my heart, I wouldn't have been thinking about Tessa for a second. I didn't love Tessa. But I did love Annisha. Desperately.

I stayed at Ronnie's house that night. Before I crawled into bed, I sent three messages. One to Annisha and Adam. One to Annisha alone. And a final one to Tessa: *Sorry,* it said.

I WOKE UP THE NEXT MORNING, just as the sun peeked through the bedroom curtains. The house was quiet, so I pulled on my clothes, grabbed my journal and tiptoed down the hall, out the door, into the backyard. Like their neighbors, Ronnie and her husband had planted a perimeter of grass around the yard. But it had gone dormant in the heat, and the dry wide blades felt rough against my bare feet. I sat down at the picnic table and gazed across the desert that stretched for miles in front of me. I could see sagebrush and boulders dotting the dry, hard earth; and here and there, a dusty juniper tree or a clump of grass.

I had one last, long leg of the trip in front of me. Julian had sent me a message saying that I would leave the Phoenix airport later that morning and head to Delhi, India. *India.* I wondered if he was going to send me to visit the monks of Sivana myself, but he had written back: *No, Jonathan, you have been on the road long enough. Just a couple of days more and you will be home.*

I opened my notebook and began to write. This journey had been to collect some mystical artifacts for my cousin. That part of it wasn't over, I knew. I had one more to pick up. But for me, the personal journey that I realized I'd undertaken felt done. I knew what I had to do. To be true to myself, I had to face my fears and ask for a transfer back to the lab or find another position. I would have to get back to the place where I could do my very best, my "genius level" work. But that was only one small aspect of the change I needed to make. I had to rebuild my world with Annisha, find a way to make up for my past neglect and renew our relationship. I had to devote myself to being the best parent I could be to Adam, and I had to stop robbing myself of the joys of spending time with my son. In fact, I had to stop robbing myself of the happiness and the positive influences of all the people dear to me—my mother, my sister, my old friends, my new ones. Ayame's talisman letter was so right—the way I had been treating others was the way I had been treating myself. By neglecting them, I had turned my back on my own happiness. I had not been kind to anyone. I would have to choose my influences better in the future. I would have to celebrate all the simple pleasures available to me. None of this would happen overnight. But I would work on it each day, live each day as if it were my whole life in miniature. Small daily improvements. No excuses.

I felt as if I had all the tools I needed to move into the future. The talisman letters had given these to me. What could be left, I wondered? What other wisdom could that last talisman impart?

## CHAPTER ELEVEN

I WAS STANDING OUTSIDE the most magnificent building I had ever seen—the Taj Mahal. It was dusk, and the visitors and tourists were emptying from the place. It seemed like an odd time to meet someone here, but nothing about this trip had been expected.

Before I had left the Phoenix airport, Julian had sent me a message with detailed instructions. I would stay overnight in Delhi, checking into a hotel. The next day, I would take a flight to Agra, where I would meet the final safekeeper outside the Taj Mahal at seven-thirty p.m. The thought of navigating around Delhi and Agra on my own, on such short notice, would have unnerved me just a few weeks ago. But I had been to so many places, experienced so many different things lately, that I felt a new confidence in facing the challenges that came my way. And now, all thoughts of the past and the future were being swept away as I stood on the Taj Mahal plaza looking up at the mausoleum.

I had come here a little early, thinking I might go inside and look around on my own before the Taj Mahal closed for the day. But once I arrived, I realized how foolish I was to think I could properly see anything so spectacular in such a short period of time. Julian had not yet told me when I would be leaving Agra. I was hoping there would be time to come back to explore this breathtaking architectural masterwork more fully. In the meantime I wandered around the exterior of the monument, my head back and my mouth agape.

I was simply overwhelmed by the size of the place. Nothing in any of the photos I had seen had managed to convey the enormity of the building, the sinuous dome, the elegant symmetry, the extraordinary expanses. Now I could see why Julian had set up this meeting for the evening. The setting sun made the color of these luminescent walls of marble and sandstone shift and dance. As I moved closer I could see that the outside surfaces were covered in intricate stone carvings and delicate calligraphy that reached a hundred feet skyward. Precious gems and stones embroidered the lacy stone: I could see bits of turquoise, lapis lazuli, emerald, red coral. I walked back and forth in front the building, moving close to examine the exquisite details and then stepping back to take in the incredible grandeur.

I had been walking around the Taj Mahal, deeply immersed in the moment, completely forgetting why I was there, when a flash of crimson caught my eye. I turned around. In front of me was a tall figure. Even though the person was facing away from me, I could tell it was a man. He stood motionless, the robe that adorned his slender frame flapping slightly in the breeze. He then spun around. And flashed a smile. It was Julian.

"What?" I sputtered. None of this made sense. What was Julian doing here? Why hadn't he told me that he was coming to India? And if he was here to pick up the talismans himself, why did he have me fly all this way?

"I'm here to take those talismans off your hands," Julian said with a wink.

My jaw was working, trying to form the words to all the questions that were racing through my head.

"I know," said Julian. "This is a long way for you to come when I am already here. But I'm on my way to the Himalayas for a while. This was really the best place to meet."

I nodded, still in a fog of shock and confusion.

"Let's head down there," said Julian, pointing to the long flower-and-tree-lined avenues that banked the reflecting pool. "Find a place to sit, perhaps . . . in the evening air."

We left the archways of the Taj Mahal and headed down the stone steps. The water in the pools was getting dark, the sun dipping below the horizon, the sky a soft shade of indigo.

As we walked, Julian slipped his hand into a pocket of his robe.

"Would you like to see the last talisman?" he asked.

"You have it with you?" I said.

Julian nodded and then pulled out a small brown bag. I held out my hand, and he emptied the bag into my palm. I was holding a tiny marble replica of the Taj Mahal. There was no parchment or note of any sort. I cocked my head.

"Let me explain what this means," said Julian. "This last talisman is all about legacy," he said. "The monks say that the best way to evaluate someone's greatness is to look at the strength of that person's influence on the generation that will follow. So if we are truly interested in rising into rare air as human beings, instead of 'what's in it for me?' we should be asking 'what's in it for the world?' That is why the Taj Mahal is the perfect symbol for legacy."

I looked back at the ethereal structure. It was shimmering pink, radiating as if it were itself a glittering star.

"Yes, I can see that," I said. "This building has inspired and influenced so many dreamers from so many places. For hundreds of years. I can't quite believe it is the work of one man. That it was built in one lifetime."

"There's no doubt about it," said Julian. "This is a remarkable work of art, or architecture. Few people leave something of such beauty and significance behind. But when I think of the legacy of the Taj Mahal's creator, it is not really architecture I think of."

I looked at Julian, uncertain about what he was trying to say.

"Let me tell you the story of the Taj Mahal," said Julian.

Shah Jahan was the emperor of the Moghul Empire in the early 1600s, Julian explained. His wife was a woman he called Mumtaz Mahal, or Jewel of the Palace. He adored her, and she him. Tragically, Mumtaz Mahal died while giving birth to her fourteenth child. According to the legend, Mumtaz's last words to her husband spoke of their everlasting love.

Shah Jahan was devastated by her death. After a year of mourning in reclusion and rejecting earthly pleasures, Jahan decided to spend his life honoring his beloved by building her a resting place that would be a heaven on earth. And every year, between two and four million people come to see what Shah Jahan constructed for the love of his life.

"Not many of us will leave the world something on the scale of the Taj Mahal," Julian said. "But even more modest contributions are still precious contributions."

Julian began digging around in the pocket of his robe. He pulled out a small piece of parchment and handed it to me. It read:

*Stand for Something Bigger than Yourself*

*There are no extra people alive today. Every single one of us is here for a reason, a special purpose—a mission. Yes, build a beautiful life for yourself and those you love. Yes, be happy and have a lot of fun. And yes, become successful, on your own terms rather than on those suggested to you by society. But—above all else—be significant. Make your life matter. Be of use. And be of service to as many people as possible. This is how each of us can shift from the realm of the ordinary into the heights of the extraordinary. And walk among the best who have ever lived.*

"It made a big difference that Mumtaz Mahal lived," Julian said quietly. "Her shadow is even longer than her husband's. It was her love that led to all this." Julian's hand swept in front of him.

"Sometimes, Jonathan," Julian continued, "our contributions are clearly visible to the world—an advancement in science, a work of art, the creation of a successful company, the building of a house or a city. But sometimes our contributions are less tangible, less measurable. What is important is that we *do* contribute. That we make a difference. That we leave a legacy."

I could see now that I had been wrong in Sedona. There had been a piece of missing wisdom in that collection of talismans. Legacy. It was not about making money or receiving applause. It was, it seemed, about influence and impact, about making the world a better place. Li Gao understood that. My sister, Kira, understood that. My father and mother understood that. And sitting here in front of this inspiring memorial to love, I knew it was something I would think about for days and years to come. What would my legacy be? What difference would I make?

"Now," said Julian after a few moments of silence. "Do you have the talismans?"

"Oh," I said. "I almost forgot."

That wasn't quite true. The fact was that I found myself curiously reluctant to part with them.

As I lifted my shirt and slowly untied the pouch from my belt loop, Julian smiled.

"You've become a little attached to them," said Julian kindly. "You've discovered their power."

"Well, I don't know," I said.

"I think you must have. How are you feeling?" Julian asked.

"Good," I said. "Surprisingly good."

"No jetlag? No fatigue? Lots of energy?"

"Yeah," I said slowly. "Do you think . . . ?"

"The wisdom of these talismans, if you embrace it, if you commit yourself to it, can change your life. As I told you earlier, it can be *lifesaving.*"

"About that," I said, remembering my mother's tearful voice so many weeks ago, "who is in danger? Whose life are you trying to save with these things?"

Julian looked at me with raised eyebrows but said nothing. There was a moment of silence as the truth washed over me.

"Oh come on," I said, my face growing hot. "I'm not in danger. My life doesn't need saving."

Julian didn't say anything. But he continued to look at me as if waiting for something. The talismans were still in my hand.

"I'm a healthy guy with a great kid, and, okay, a marriage that needs a bit of work but. . ."

"Jonathan, you know as well as I do that your life was in trouble. Your mother could see that, and she was sick with worry. She had lost your father, and she felt she was losing you, too. She could see that you were never going to find the happiness and contentment that she and your dad had if you continued the way you were going. You were working in a job you hated; you squandered your marriage; and you were missing the childhood of your son."

"So all this talisman stuff was just nonsense? There was no magic cure?"

"The real magic was in those letters, Jonathan, in those letters and in your journal. The talismans provided a way to get you to pay attention. The journey was the way to give you time to absorb the lessons that the letters—and my friends—shared with you.

"Jonathan, you were willing to work hard, to face your fears, to take risks to save someone else's life. But when you started out, you weren't willing to do those things to save your own. I think, however, that now you are."

"But what about all the safekeepers?" I asked. "Do they know that there isn't any magic to these things—even if you have all of them in one place?"

Julian smiled. "That was my only real dishonesty, Jonathan.

I collected these little amulets after I spoke with your mother a few months ago, and then I mailed them off to my friends. They understood what was going on, and they were happy to help. Each one of those people is wise in their own way—to me they epitomize the knowledge that was in each of those letters. I have learned so much from each of them, and I wanted you to meet them and learn from them, too. And this was the only way I could think to do it. You never would have gone otherwise."

I had enjoyed meeting these friends of Julian's, and I had to confess that I would have liked to spend more time with each of them. That made me think of the people I couldn't spend more time with—my father. And Juan.

Julian pointed to a little stone bench ahead of us. As we sat down, he put his hand gently on my shoulder.

"I think that many things are clear to you now, but something is still bothering you," he said gently.

I had been brooding about all this for so long it was hard to know where to start the story. So I started at the beginning. I told Julian all about working with Juan in the lab, about my decision to leave. I explained how Sven and David had been trying to force Juan to quit, how I had neither defended him nor even provided friendship or sympathy. Then I told him about Juan's car crash.

"An accident," said Julian. He said it matter-of-factly, but there was the hint of a question in his voice.

When I didn't say anything, he continued. "But you are doubtful."

"Yes," I said finally. "Juan had a heart attack. That much is certain. But when did he have it? Before or after he crashed through the guardrail?"

Julian looked at me sadly, as if he knew my story hadn't reached its conclusion.

I looked down at the stones in front of me, the great dome in the distance.

"Two days before he died," I continued, "I walked past Juan's office. He was coming out the door. He was looking at his feet, clearly lost in thought. He almost bumped into me. When he saw me, his expression didn't change. He spoke as if he wasn't really addressing me, was just continuing his private thoughts out loud.

"'There hardly seems any point in going on' is what Juan said. At the time, I thought he was talking about quitting. And as shameful as it is to admit, I was relieved. At least I wouldn't have to see his harrowed face each day. At least I could pretend that things would turn out for the best. I didn't say anything to Juan, and he continued past me, down the hall, his head lowered and his steps heavy. But after . . . Juan's words ate away at me like acid. Had those words foretold the fatal crash? Was Juan deciding to end his life, not his career? And if I had stopped him, talked with him, offered my help or my sympathy, might he still be alive today?"

Julian and I were both quiet for a while. There were only a few people in sight. The emptiness of the place seemed surreal after the noisy, crowded streets of Delhi and Agra.

Julian clasped his hands and stretched his legs in front of him. His brown leather sandals peeked out from under his crimson robe.

"Jonathan," he began. "I like to say that what we all need to do is look ahead five years and predict what things in our current life we will most regret. Then we must take actions *today* to prevent those regrets from being realized."

Julian reached out and put his hand over mine.

"I think, during this trip, you have probably started that process. I think your future is going to look very different from how it would have turned out if you hadn't undergone this journey. But that is the future. What you are talking about now is the past. You know as well as I do that no one will ever be able to answer those questions you are asking. And you must be brave enough to accept that."

I sighed deeply. I was hoping that Julian's answer would be different, but I knew it wouldn't be.

"You can't move forward while looking back, Jonathan," said Julian firmly. "And there is nothing you can do to change the past."

"But I feel as if I should do something to make amends, to show how sorry I am," I said.

"There are two things you can do," said Julian. I looked up at him, feeling for the first time hopeful about this.

"Two things you *must* do," Julian continued. "First is make sure that you never neglect a friend that way again; that you don't bear silent witness to the cruelty and bad behavior of others."

I nodded. I had already made that resolution to myself months ago.

"And second," Julian continued, "you must forgive yourself."

Julian was looking at me intently.

"Do you remember the crane talisman, Jonathan?"

"Yes," I said, thinking fondly of Ayame.

"Do you remember what that letter said about the importance of treating others kindly, and treating yourself the same way? It is important that you forgive others. It is *essential* that you forgive yourself."

I ran my hands down my legs. I knew Julian was right. It might be the hardest thing I've ever had to do, but I had to stop wallowing in regret. I had to let it go. And move on.

"And speaking of forgiveness," said Julian. He was standing up. "There is someone else who would like to see you."

The sun had now disappeared completely, leaving only a faint glow along the horizon. The moon was bright in the sky, hanging like a golden coin against a deep bank of velvet. I looked around. Light was sparkling off the water in the reflecting pool, but the garden was dark and empty. Then I noticed a small figure at the edge of the stone avenue . . . walking toward me. I looked over at Julian, but he was gone. When I turned back, the moonlight revealed the figure of a woman: petite and slender; long, dark hair disappearing behind her shoulders. She was close enough now that I could see the smile spreading across her face. Annisha! My heart leaped and I sprang to my feet.

Then, as I moved toward her, I saw something else. The tiny figure of my son appeared just behind his mother. Adam put his head down and pumped his arms as he raced past Annisha. I stooped down with my arms open to receive him. All I could manage to say was his name before tears choked my voice.


ANNISHA, ADAM AND I stayed in Agra for three days before heading back home. The time we spent together in India felt like the most important thing I had ever done.

Julian told me to keep the talismans—and the letters. "Perhaps someday," he said, "you will want to give the talismans to

Adam and teach him everything you have learned from them." The thought of that made me smile.

WHEN I RETURNED TO WORK after my long absence, it was to a sea of new faces, and to an office without David, or Sven for that matter. I spent a long time talking with various managers and the new CEO. A lot of people, including my clients, tried to talk me into staying in sales. But I knew where I would do my best work. Eventually they agreed, and after several months as acting technical director, they gave me the post permanently.

Of course, before all of that unfolded, I got rid of the apartment and moved back in with Annisha and Adam. Adam immediately started a campaign to get me to be an assistant coach for his soccer team. He seemed surprised at how quickly I agreed. And Annisha and I started on the slow, careful work of rebuilding our marriage.

One of the first things we did was institute a new tradition— a once-a-month Sunday dinner with my mother, my sister and her family, and Annisha's parents. And we started to plan our next vacation.

"Where shall we go?" asked Annisha, as she sat looking at some of the travel books my mother had lent us. "Who should we see?"

"Let's start at the beginning," I suggested, thinking fondly of my new life and my new friends. "Let's start with Istanbul."

# THE TALISMAN LETTERS

### *The Power of Authenticity*
The most important gift we can give ourselves is the commitment to living our authentic life. To be true to ourselves, however, is not an easy task. We must break free of the seductions of society and live life on our own terms, under our own values and aligned with our original dreams. We must tap our hidden selves; explore the deep-seated, unseen hopes, desires, strengths and weaknesses that make us who we are. We have to understand where we have been and know where we are going. Every decision we make, every step we take, must be informed by our commitment to living a life that is true and honest and authentic to ourselves and ourselves alone. And as we proceed, we are certain to experience fortune well beyond our highest imagination.

### *Embrace Your Fears*
What holds us back in life is the invisible architecture of fear. It keeps us in our comfort zones, which are, in truth, the least safe places in which to live. Indeed, the greatest risk in life is taking no risks. But every time we do that which we fear, we take back the power that fear has stolen from us—for on the other side of our fears lives our strength. Every time we step into the discomfort of growth and progress, we become more free. The more fears we walk through, the more power we reclaim. In this way, we grow both fearless and powerful, and thus are able to live the lives of our dreams.

### Live with Kindness

It is important to remember that just as our words are our thoughts verbalized, so our deeds are our beliefs actualized. No action, no matter how small, is insignificant—how we treat someone defines how we treat everyone, including ourselves. If we disrespect another, we disrespect ourselves. If we are mistrustful of others, we are distrustful of ourselves. If we are cruel to another, we will be cruel to ourselves. If we can't appreciate those around us, we won't appreciate ourselves. With every person we engage, in everything we do, we must be kinder than expected, more generous than anticipated, more positive than we thought possible. Every moment in front of another human being is an opportunity to express our highest values and to influence someone with our humanity. We can make the world better, one person at a time.

### Make Small Daily Progress

The way we do small things determines the way that we do everything. If we execute our minor tasks well, we will also excel at our larger efforts. Mastery then becomes our way of being. But more than this—each tiny effort builds on the next, so that brick by brick, magnificent things can be created, great confidence grows and uncommon dreams are realized. The truly wise recognize that small daily improvements always lead to exceptional results over time.

### To Lead Your Best Life, Do Your Best Work

There is no insignificant work in the world. All labor is a chance to express personal talents, to create our art and to realize the genius we are built to be. We must work like Picasso painted: with devotion, passion, energy and excellence. In this way, our productivity will not only become a source of inspiration to others, but it will have an impact—making a difference in the lives around us. One of the greatest secrets to a life beautifully lived is to do work that matters. And to ascend to such a state of mastery in it that people can't take their eyes off of you.

### Choose Your Influences Well

We do not move through our days alone or apart from the world around us. And so we must always be aware of the things and the people we allow into our lives. It's a mark of wisdom to choose to spend time in those places that inspire and energize you and associate with those people who elevate and uplift you. Whether in our work or within our personal lives, these most positive friends and peers will inspire us to be our greatest selves and to lead our largest lives.

### Life's Simplest Pleasures Are Life's Greatest Joys.

Most people don't discover what's most important in life until they are too old to do anything about it. They spend many of their best years pursuing things that matter little in the end. While society invites us to fill our lives with material objects, the best part of us knows that the more basic pleasures are the ones that enrich and sustain us. No matter how easy or hard our current conditions, we all have a wealth of simple blessings around us—waiting to be counted. As we do, our happiness grows. Our gratitude expands. And each day becomes a breathtaking gift.

### The Purpose of Life Is to Love

How well you live comes down to how much you love. The heart is wiser than the head. Honor it. Trust it. Follow it.

### Stand for Something Bigger than Yourself

There are no extra people alive today. Every single one of us is here for a reason, a special purpose—a mission. Yes, build a beautiful life for yourself and those you love. Yes, be happy and have a lot of fun. And yes, become successful, on your own terms rather than on those suggested to you by society. But— above all else—be significant. Make your life matter—be of use. And be of service to as many people as possible. This is how each of us can shift from the realm of the ordinary into the heights of the extraordinary. And walk among the best who have ever lived.

Also by Robin Sharma and available
from HarperElement

Over 3 Million Copies Sold

# ROBIN SHARMA

# THE MONK
# WHO SOLD
# HIS FERRARI

'A captivating story
that teaches as it delights'
PAULO COELHO, *THE ALCHEMIST*

From the International Bestselling Author
# ROBIN SHARMA

## DISCOVER YOUR DESTINY

with the Monk Who Sold His Ferrari

The 7 Stages of Self-Awakening

From the International Bestselling Author
# ROBIN SHARMA

# LEADERSHIP
# WISDOM
## from the Monk Who
## Sold His Ferrari
## The 8 Rituals of
## The Best Leaders

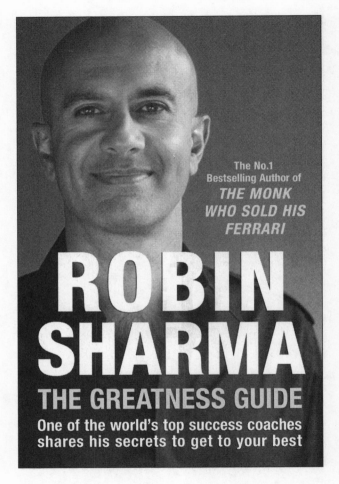

The No.1
Bestselling Author of
*THE MONK
WHO SOLD HIS
FERRARI*

# ROBIN
# SHARMA

## THE GREATNESS GUIDE

One of the world's top success coaches
shares his secrets to get to your best

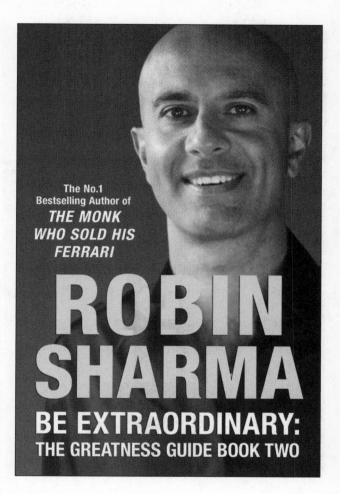

The No.1
Bestselling Author of
*THE MONK
WHO SOLD HIS
FERRARI*

# ROBIN
# SHARMA

## BE EXTRAORDINARY:
### THE GREATNESS GUIDE BOOK TWO